How to Use This Book

CliffsNotes Sinclair's *The Jungle* supplements the original work, giving you background information about the author, an introduction to the novel, a graphical character map, critical commentaries, expanded glossaries, and a comprehensive index. CliffsNotes Review tests your comprehension of the original text and reinforces learning with questions and answers, practice projects, and more. For further information on Upton Sinclair and *The Jungle*, check out the CliffsNotes Resource Center.

CliffsNotes provides the following icons to highlight essential elements of particular interest:

Reveals the underlying themes in the work.

Helps you to more easily relate to or discover the depth of a character.

Highlights elements such as setting, atmosphere, mystery, passion, violence, irony, symbolism, tragedy, foreshadowing, and satire.

Enables you to appreciate the nuances of words and phrases.

Don't Miss Our Web Site

Discover classic literature as well as modern-day treasures by visiting the Cliffs Notes Web site at www.cliffsnotes.com. You can obtain a quick download of a CliffsNotes title, purchase a title in print form, browse our catalog, and view online samples.

You also find fun and informative interactive tools, links to interesting Web sites, tips, articles, and additional resources to help you, not only for literature, but for test prep, finance, careers, computers, and Internet too. See you at www.cliffsnotes.com!

CliffsNotes™

Sinclair's
The Jungle

By Richard Wasowski, M.A.

IN THIS BOOK

- Probe the Life and Background of the Author
- Preview the novel in the Introduction to the Novel
- Discover the themes in the Critical Commentaries
- Examine in-depth Character Analyses
- Explore the significance of the work with Critical Essays
- Reinforce what you learn with CliffsNotes Review
- Find additional information to further your study in CliffsNotes Resource Center and online at www.cliffsnotes.com

IDG Books Worldwide, Inc.
An International Data Group Company
Foster City, CA • Chicago, IL • Indianapolis, IN • New York, NY

About the Author
   Richard Wasowski earned his M.A. from Ohio State University and teaches secondary English in Ashland.
Publisher's Acknowledgments
Editorial
   Project Editor: Kathleen A. Dobie
   Acquisitions Editor: Gregory W. Tubach
   Copy Editor: Rowena Rappaport

Glossary Editors: The editors and staff at Webster's New World™ Dictionaries
Editorial Administrator: Michelle Hacker
Editorial Assistant: Jennifer Young
Production
Indexer: York Production Services, Inc.
Proofreader: York Production Services, Inc.
IDG Books Indianapolis Production Department

CliffsNotes™ Sinclair's *The Jungle*
Published by
IDG Books Worlwide, Inc.
An International Data Group Company
919 E. Hillsdale Blvd.
Suite 300
Foster City, CA 94404
www.idgbooks.com (IDG Books Worldwide Web site)
www.cliffsnotes.com (CliffsNotes Web site)

Library of Congress Control Number: 00-107701

ISBN: 0-7645-8675-0

Printed in the United States of America

10 9 8 7 6 5 4 3 2 1

1O/SQ/RR/QQ/IN

Distributed in the United States by Hungry Minds, Inc.

Distributed by CDG Books Canada Inc. for Canada; by Transworld Publishers Limited in the United Kingdom; by IDG Norge Books for Norway; by IDG Sweden Books for Sweden; by IDG Books Australia Publishing Corporation Pty. Ltd. for Australia and New Zealand; by Trans-Quest Publishers Pte Ltd. for Singapore, Malaysia, Thailand, Indonesia, and Hong Kong; by Gotop Information Inc. for Taiwan; by ICG Muse, Inc. for Japan; by Norma Comunicaciones S.A. for Columbia; by Intersoft for South Africa; by Eyrolles for France; by International Thomson Publishing for Germany, Austria and Switzerland; by Distribuidora Cuspide for Argentina; by LR International for Brazil; by Galileo Libros for Chile; by Ediciones ZETA S.C.R. Ltda. for Peru; by WS Computer Publishing Corporation, Inc., for the Philippines; by Contemporanea de Ediciones for Venezuela; by Express Computer Distributors for the Caribbean and West Indies; by Micronesia Media Distributor, Inc. for Micronesia; by Grupo Editorial Norma S.A. for Guatemala; by Chips Computadoras S.A. de C.V. for Mexico; by Editorial Norma de Panama S.A. for Panama; by American Bookshops for Finland. Authorized Sales Agent: Anthony Rudkin Associates for the Middle East and North Africa.

For general information on IDG Books Worlwide's books in the U.S., please call our Consumer Customer Service department at **800-762-2974**. For reseller information, including discounts and premium sales, please call our Reseller Customer Service department at **800-434-3422.**

For information on where to purchase IDG Books Worldwide's books outside the U.S., please contact our International Sales department at **317-572-3993** or fax **317-572-4002.**

For consumer information on foreign language translations, please contact our Customer Service department at **1-800-434-3422,** fax **317-572-4002,** or e-mail rights@idgbooks.com.

For information on licensing foreign or domestic rights, please phone **+1-650-653-7098.**

For sales inquiries and special prices for bulk quantities, please contact our Order Services department at **800-434-3422** or write to the address above.

For information on using IDG Books Worldwide's books in the classroom or for ordering examination copies, please contact our Educational Sales department at **800-434-2086** or fax **317-572-4005.**

For press review copies, author interviews, or other publicity information, please contact our Public Relations department at **650-653-7000** or fax **650-653-7500.**

For authorization to photocopy items for corporate, personal, or educational use, please contact Copyright Clearance Center, 222 Rosewood Drive, Danvers, MA 01923, or fax **978-750-4470.**

is a registered trademark under exclusive license to IDG Books Worldwide, Inc. from International Data Group, Inc.

Table of Contents

Life and Background of the Author 1
Personal Background 2
Literary Career 3
Political Background 4
Career Highlights 5

Introduction to the Novel 7
Introduction 8
List of Characters 11
Character Map 14

Critical Commentaries 15
Chapter 1 16
   Summary 16
   Commentary 16
   Glossary 19
Chapter 2 20
   Summary 20
   Commentary 20
   Glossary 21
Chapter 3 22
   Summary 22
   Commentary 22
   Glossary 23
Chapter 4 24
   Summary 24
   Commentary 24
   Glossary 25
Chapter 5 26
   Summary 26
   Commentary 26
   Glossary 27
Chapter 6 28
   Summary 28
   Commentary 28
   Glossary 29
Chapter 7 30
   Summary 30
   Commentary 30
   Glossary 31

Chapter 8 32
   Summary 32
   Commentary 32
   Glossary 32
Chapter 9 34
   Summary 34
   Commentary 34
   Glossary 35
Chapter 10 36
   Summary 36
   Commentary 36
   Glossary 37
Chapter 11 38
   Summary 38
   Commentary 38
   Glossary 39
Chapter 12 40
   Summary 40
   Commentary 40
   Glossary 40
Chapter 13 41
   Summary 41
   Commentary 41
   Glossary 42
Chapter 14 43
   Summary 43
   Commentary 43
   Glossary 44
Chapter 15 45
   Summary 45
   Commentary 45
   Glossary 46
Chapter 16 47
   Summary 47
   Commentary 47
   Glossary 47
Chapter 17 48
   Summary 48
   Commentary 48
   Glossary 49

Chapter 18 50
    Summary 50
    Commentary 50
    Glossary 50
Chapter 19 51
    Summary 51
    Commentary 51
    Glossary 51
Chapter 20 53
    Summary 53
    Commentary 53
    Glossary 53
Chapter 21 55
    Summary 55
    Commentary 55
    Glossary 56
Chapter 22 57
    Summary 57
    Commentary 57
    Glossary 57
Chapter 23 58
    Summary 58
    Commentary 58
    Glossary 58
Chapter 24 59
    Summary 59
    Commentary 59
    Glossary 59
Chapter 25 61
    Summary 61
    Commentary 61
    Glossary 62
Chapter 26 63
    Summary 63
    Commentary 63
    Glossary 64
Chapter 27 65
    Summary 65
    Commentary 65
    Glossary 66

Chapter 28 67
  Summary 67
  Commentary 67
  Glossary 68
Chapter 29 69
  Summary 69
  Commentary 69
  Glossary 69
Chapter 30 71
  Summary 71
  Commentary 71
  Glossary 71
Chapter 31 73
  Summary 73
  Commentary 73
  Glossary 74

Character Analyses **75**
  The Narrator 76
  Jurgis 77
  Ona 79
  Marija 80
  Elzbieta 81
  Phil Connor 81
  Jack Duane 82

Critical Essays **83**
  The Tenets of Sinclair's Socialism 84
  Jurgis' Journey through Hell to Socialism 85
  Sinclair's *The Jungle* from a Contemporary Critical Perspective 87

CliffsNotes Review **91**
  Q&A 91
  Identify the Quote 91
  Essay Questions 92
  Practice Project 92

CliffsNotes Resource Center **93**
  Books and Periodicals 93
  Internet 94
  Audio Recording 94

Index **97**

LIFE AND BACKGROUND OF THE AUTHOR

Personal Background 2

Literary Career 3

Political Background 4

Career Highlights 5

Life and Background of the Author

Although he published over 90 books throughout his 65-year literary career, and his novel *Dragon's Teeth* won the 1943 Pulitzer Prize for Fiction, Upton Sinclair is best known for his controversial and often misunderstood novel *The Jungle*. Sinclair's primary interest was in social change, and his concern for social and moral improvement dominated his prolific writings: Sinclair's novels, plays, pamphlets, and articles reflected social themes.

The honors and output would seemingly have assured Sinclair a favorable place in American literary history; however, this is not the case. Although he was extremely popular during his day, critics focused on his political ideology and did not embrace his work as receptively as the general reading public did. Historically, his peers, such as Theodore Dreiser, Frank Norris, and fellow socialist Jack London, tended to be the critical favorites, whereas Sinclair's works were often routinely dismissed. Today, *The Jungle* is the only one of his works that is widely read. The pendulum of perception continually shifts, however, and Sinclair's work is slowly creeping back into favor with contemporary critics. Contemporary scholars look beyond his political agenda when analyzing his literary efforts.

Personal Background

He was born Upton Beall Sinclair, Jr., on September 20, 1878, in Baltimore, into a relatively poor family, although his mother's family had money. Because his father's financial failures mixed with his mother's affluent family, Sinclair was able to experience two diverse lifestyles. As his father continued to face hardships, he succumbed to the temptation of liquor. Sinclair's distaste for alcohol is apparent in many of his works, including *The Jungle*.

Early Years

When Sinclair was 10, he moved to New York City. An advanced student and gifted writer, at 14 he entered the College of the City of New York (though called a college, it was closer to a high school) and supported himself by writing routine and often dull novels (called *hack* or *pulp fiction*) for popular magazines. Under various pseudonyms he wrote stories for boys' magazines, too. Sinclair saw himself, at this time, as a poet, embracing Jesus, Hamlet, and Percy Bysshe Shelley.

Education

While in New York, Sinclair developed his passion for moral and social justice through his relationship with Reverend W.W. Moir, an Episcopalian minister who was a strong influence during Sinclair's adolescent years. Sinclair admired Moir's abandonment of familial wealth for the clergy, and Moir served as a father figure for Sinclair. The relationship, mixed with Sinclair's study of what he considered conflicting messages in official church teachings, resulted in Sinclair's lifelong following of the moral teachings of Jesus while having little use for organized religion. He earned his B.A. from City College of New York in 1897 and subsequently entered a graduate program at Columbia University.

Literary Career

In 1900, Sinclair left his graduate program to write a poetic novel, and later that year married Meta Fuller. This novel, *Springtime and Harvest* (later published as *King Midas*) was published a year later, the same year his first son, David was born. During the next three years, he continued writing pulp fiction and worked as a journalist to support his family. These jobs, combined with his interest in socialism, conflicted with his desire to be a poet. Sinclair wanted to use words and language to express universal ideals and truths, but instead he found himself using words and language to amuse, entertain, and pay the bills. He recognized that the life of a poet was not always the life of practicality, but having a wife and son to support, Sinclair needed to be practical and abandoned the life of a poet.

The editor of *Appeal to Reason*, Fred D. Warren, read *Manassas* (1904), Sinclair's third novel, and commissioned Sinclair to write about the conditions of the Chicago stockyards for the *Appeal*, a weekly socialist newspaper. After accepting the assignment, Sinclair lived in Chicago for nearly two months, studying the people and the working conditions of the industrial town. His observations became *The Jungle*, his next serious novel. After being published as a series in the *Appeal*, it took the work and financing of fellow socialist and author Jack London to get privately bound versions of the text printed. While Sinclair was publishing his book privately, five publishers rejected it based on content. Some wanted to print the book, provided that Sinclair delete some inflammatory and offensive passages. He refused. Eventually, Doubleday, Page and Company agreed to publish it, after verifying the basic truth of his allegations.

Throughout his career, Sinclair continued to write literature that depicted social issues: *Oil!* (1927) focused on the illegal leasing of oil reserves known as the Teapot Dome scandal and *The Brass Check* (1919) is a fictional account of his demonstration and subsequent arrest for speaking out against the 1914 coal mine strike. The extent of the prestige that Sinclair enjoyed during his lifetime is revealed in his 1960 collection of correspondence, *My Lifetime in Letters*. Included in the compilation are letters from Sinclair Lewis, Theodore Roosevelt, Jack London, H.L. Mencken, and Albert Einstein. Sinclair's career concluded with his final publication, *The Autobiography of Upton Sinclair*.

Political Background

The publication of *The Jungle* thrust Sinclair into the national limelight. For the first time in his career, a serious work of fiction made money for him. Sinclair's one major disappointment about his novel's reception was that *The Jungle* did not ignite the public into a frenzy over socialism.

Sinclair used his earnings to establish Helicon Hall, a commune for writers in Englewood, New Jersey. Helicon Hall was to be the epitome of cooperation, where people would live day to day looking out for the best interests of one another while simultaneously pursuing individual interests. Less than a year into its existence, Helicon burned to the ground, and Sinclair abandoned the project.

In 1908, Sinclair founded a socialist theatre to provide a site for the performance of plays with socialist messages, including his own. He continued to write a number of books, though none captured the fancy of the reading public and most were privately printed. His marriage, which was essentially a sham, continued to be a distraction to Sinclair's writing, and he tried to divorce his wife, but the courts refused his request, so Sinclair moved to Europe. The loss of Helicon Hall, combined with his inability to resolve his differences with his wife, pushed Sinclair harder to pursue a divorce. He later provided a fictional account of his marriage in the novel *Love's Pilgrimage* (1911). In Europe, he wrote two novels and finally received a divorce in 1911 with little difficulty.

Sinclair married again in 1913; his bride was Mary Craig Kimbrough. The same year, he returned to the United States, continued to write, and remained politically active. In 1915, he moved to California where he continued his writing and attempted to establish a political career. In 1923, he founded the Southern California branch of the American Civil Liberties Union.

He was the socialist candidate for one of California's seats in the House of Representatives in 1920. Two years later, on the same ticket, he was unsuccessful in his attempt to become a U.S. senator. Three times he ran for governor of California: 1926, 1930, and 1934. His most nearly successful attempt was the only time he ran on the democratic ticket (1934). His platform became known as the EPIC (End Poverty in California) plan. He had an early lead in the polls, but Sinclair had alienated himself from the powers in Hollywood because he criticized their methods and because he was seen as a communist. This prompted an organized effort by production studios, led by MGM Pictures, to defeat Sinclair.

Sinclair's switch from socialist to left-wing democrat was a gradual change. Before the United States' involvement in World War I, Sinclair alienated himself from many of his colleagues because, unlike most American socialists, he favored America's entry into the war, mostly because of the German occupation of France. Later he resigned from the Socialist Party when the official position became one of pacifism. His reaction to socialism mirrored his reaction to organized religion— belief in the ideals but not in the execution of those ideals.

Career Highlights

Sinclair's post-World War I period was a combination of an incredible outlay of writing as well as the aforementioned political activisim. In 1927, *Oil!* was published. Often considered his most effective piece of writing, *Oil!*, according to critics, illustrated a mark of maturity in Sinclair's writing. Just like the author, the protagonist of the novel rejected the ideals of World War I and was a religious cynic. *Oil!*, like the majority of Sinclair's fiction, currently is not widely available nor widely read.

During his lifetime, Sinclair received a more generous critical reception abroad than in his homeland. His work was translated into several languages and served, for many Europeans, as an information center about life in the United States. Sir Arthur Conan Doyle, of Sherlock Holmes fame, considered Sinclair one of the world's great novelists. In 1932, Sinclair was a finalist for the Nobel Prize in Literature, although he did not win the award.

Sinclair continued to print most of his novels privately until Viking Press published the Lanny Budd series in the 1940s and 1950s. This series was extremely popular and had a critical following, too. The most respected book in the series was *Dragon's Teeth* (1942), which chronicled the rise of Nazism in Germany and won the Pulitzer Prize for Fiction. The protagonist in the series—Lanny Budd—is the illegitimate son of a munitions tycoon and witnesses or figures in almost every crucial historical event in a 30-year period, a precursor to the Forrest Gump. Sinclair thought this series of literary history could serve as the texts for school children, but that did not occur.

Sinclair moved to Arizona in 1953 and continued to write. The following year his second wife died. Later that year he married his third wife, Mary Elizabeth Willis. After his wedding, Sinclair published *The Autobiography of Upton Sinclair*. Willis died in 1967, and on November 25, 1968, Sinclair died. For most of the latter part of the twentieth century, Sinclair was not widely read, primarily because literature with themes of social-change was not regarded as quality literature. Many critics felt that quality literature comments on the human condition but does not explicitly advocate change. That perception may be changing. But even if Upton Sinclair's reputation as an important and significant literary figure does not gain widespread acceptance, *The Jungle* will undoubtedly remain an American classic.

INTRODUCTION TO THE NOVEL

Introduction 8

List of Characters 11

Character Map 14

Introduction to the Novel

"I aimed for the public's heart, and by accident I hit it in the stomach." Upton Sinclair used those words to describe the reaction his novel, *The Jungle*, received upon its initial publication. Sinclair intended to illustrate the plight of immigrants in Chicago at the turn of the century; providing details and examples of abuses in the meatpacking industry merely as a means of demonstrating their troubles. Instead of being one example of many hardships, those examples, revealed in fewer than twelve pages, became both the rallying cry for industrial abuse and the public perception of the entire thematic nature of the novel.

Originally, *The Jungle* appeared in serial form in the socialist newspaper *Appeal to Reason* in 1905. Sinclair was hired to write an exposé about labor conditions in the Chicago stockyards. Sinclair's novel had mass appeal and led to an outcry against the meatpacking industry.

The harsh realities and controversial topics of *The Jungle* made finding a publisher for a bound edition difficult. Only after investigating the allegations in Sinclair's book did Doubleday, Page, and Company agree to print the book in 1906.

While publishers debated printing *The Jungle*, the public demanded government intervention against the atrocities. This public outcry led to the 1906 Meat Inspection Act and the Pure Food and Drug Act. It also, however, led to a report issued the same year by the Department of Agriculture's Bureau of Animal Husbandry that refuted the worst of Sinclair's allegations. The public's perception at this time was that the meatpacking industry feared these Acts. What was unrecognized, however, was the fact that meatpackers knew they were viewed with contempt, and facing substantial losses, the industry actually supported the Acts. They just did not want to be the ones to pay for the implementation. These Acts allayed most fears, and ironically, actually favored big business, which was the opposite of Sinclair's intention.

No one knows exactly the extent of what is fact and what is fiction in *The Jungle*. Abuse in business and government most certainly existed, for graft was a way of life. In all probability, *The Jungle* illustrates a world that was not too far removed from the reality of the day; however, the extreme examples of abuse are most likely the result of Sinclair's imagination.

Sinclair needed to include these extreme examples because he had a particular agenda when writing *The Jungle*. After following the famous meat cutters' strike of 1904, Sinclair wrote an essay challenging the union to do something after it had lost its protest. The editor of *Appeal to Reason* answered Sinclair's challenge, hiring him to write the exposé. Sinclair visited Chicago and used the real-life situations at the stockyards to discredit the American economic system—capitalism—and to show the working men that the answer to their troubles was socialism. In fact, he dedicated his novel to the working men of America, and many editions of *The Jungle* still carry that dedication.

Naturalism

When writing his book, Sinclair used a variety of styles and influences to create essentially a new type of novel. Elements of naturalism exist throughout most of the text. *Naturalism*, as a type of literature, attempts to apply scientific principles and detachment when studying humans. The characters created in naturalistic fiction are "human beasts" who can be studied by examining their surroundings. Emile Zola provided the classical definition and application of naturalism. When Sinclair was taking copious notes about his experiences in Chicago, he was being a *naturalist practitioner*.

The literary components of character, setting, and theme are three areas where *The Jungle* exemplifies naturalistic fiction tendencies. Characters in this genre typically are lower-class people who struggle against forces beyond their control. The setting tends to be urban, and the details and examples used to show a slice of life often end up being a chronicle of despair. It is extremely important that harsh realities be portrayed as such, no matter how unsavory they may be. Only when novelists present all the facts do they finally reveal the truth. Finally, two themes dominate naturalistic novels: survival and futile attempts to exercise free will. These themes are apparent throughout *The Jungle*.

The Jungle, however, is not pure naturalism. Sinclair incorporates just enough of it to suit his rhetorical purpose. Unlike pure *Zolaism* (another name for naturalism), Sinclair's *The Jungle* is lacking in objectivity: Sinclair clearly sympathizes with the working class. Sinclair also saves Jurgis, the protagonist, from destruction. This totally undermines the pessimistic naturalistic belief in futility.

Muckraking

In addition to elements of naturalism, Sinclair incorporates a variety of muckraking techniques. The *muckrakers* were writers who used non-fiction—particularly facts, figures, and laws—to support their beliefs and reveal abuses in business and government in their publications. Muckraking novels, also known as social protest novels, exist to expose conditions that need to be changed. When muckraking novels move from exposing faults to advocating a particular method as the only means for change, they're considered propaganda. Although most critics regard *The Jungle* as propaganda, it differs from most propaganda novels whose authors readily concede bias. Sinclair considers his work more than just a means to an end; that is, he felt he was creating quality literature that simultaneously served as propaganda promoting socialism. Sinclair's political views and portrayal of life in the slums alienated many readers who were uncomfortable reading about the realities of being poor, yet only in the final four chapters of *The Jungle* does Sinclair's socialist propaganda take control of his narrative. Critics who routinely dismiss *The Jungle* as propaganda are as guilty of misreading Sinclair's work as those who consider it only a muckraking novel about the meatpacking industry.

Critical Reception

Granted, the ending of *The Jungle* reads as a treatise for socialism (it did first appear in a socialist newspaper), and scholars often dismiss Sinclair and his work instead of trying to determine his place in American literature. Very few contemporary critics consider *The Jungle* as favorably as Sinclair's socialist contemporary Jack London, who claimed that "what *Uncle Tom's Cabin* did for black slaves, *The Jungle* has a large chance to do for the wage slaves of today." The comparison to Harriet Beecher Stowe's famous book remains, and many critics think these two works deserve special consideration, not so much for their literary merit, but for the impact they had on the American public.

Still other critics recognize *The Jungle* as an early work, sort of a work in progress, for a future Pulitzer Prize winning novelist, embracing the positive aspects and forgetting the rest. Even the lukewarm responses praise Sinclair's incredible imagery and brutal realism. Thematically—the notion that industry is a jungle and the law of the jungle is survival of the fittest—Sinclair's book is as relevant at the turn of the next century as it was 100 years ago.

Contemporary critics who regard Sinclair and *The Jungle* favorably note that capitalism often times does encourage greed and ruthless competition and that many writers who state that the American dream is a myth are routinely embraced by those who reject Sinclair.

Sinclair had no models or traditions to follow, so *The Jungle* became, as critic William A. Bloodworth, Jr. states, "a flawed but strenuous effort" to create a new type of novel. Those in Sinclair's corner also claim that social indignation is a legitimate aspiration for any novelist. *The Jungle* and Sinclair have endured, not for any one particular reason, but rather, for a variety of reasons.

List of Characters

Jurgis Rudkus   The protagonist. He is a Lithuanian immigrant who believes in himself and his work ethic but finds that making a living for his wife and family takes more than hard work and dedication. He believes in the American dream and wants to make it a reality, but in the end, he discovers that he was following the wrong dream.

Ona Lukoszaite   Jurgis' fiancée and later his wife. Her frail nature—both physically and emotionally—does not lend itself towards survival in the Packingtown jungle in which she must attempt to live.

Elzbieta Lukoszaite (Teta Elzbieta)   Ona's stepmother. She endures one tragedy after another, never really living, only surviving.

Marija Berczynskas   Ona's cousin. Although the prototype of strength and endurance for most of the novel, she too is eventually defeated by the capitalistic system, although she is matter-of-fact about her fate.

Jonas   Elzbieta's brother. He comes to America with the rest of the family, but the only way he can survive is by abandoning the family and taking care of himself.

Antanas Rudkus (Dede Antanas) Jurgis' father. From the onset, he is determined to contribute to the family's success in Chicago; however, unlike in other countries, in the America he encounters the elderly are neither appreciated nor respected, and he dies destitute and deceived.

Stanislovas, Kotrina, Vilimas, Nikalojus, Juozapas, Kristoforas Elzbieta's children. Illustrating the abuse children suffered as a result of the industrial revolution, they all either die or are sent to work at much too young an age.

Antanas Rudkus (Little Antanas) Only child of Ona and Jurgis. He is Jurgis' hope for the future but he suffers a fate similar to his mother and cousins'.

Tamoszius Kuszleika A violinist. His passion for the violin exceeds his talent; for a while it seems that he and Marija might marry, but they are not destined to be together.

Jokubas Szedvilas A fellow Lithuanian immigrant. He owns a delicatessen and introduces Jurgis and his family to Packingtown.

The Widow Jukiene Jurgis' first landlady in Chicago. Twice Jurgis and his family are forced to rent "unthinkably filthy" rooms from her.

Mike Scully The democratic boss of Packingtown. Jurgis would not be so eager to work for the man if he knew the entire truth about Scully's involvement with Jurgis' family: Jurgis sees Scully as a powerful friend and ally, but actually Scully is both directly and indirectly responsible for the deaths of Ona and Little Antanas.

Phil Connor Ona's boss. He serves as a nemesis for Jurgis and illustrates the theory that might makes right. He also demonstrates that it is not what you know but who you know that counts.

Jack Duane Jurgis' cellmate. He introduces Jurgis to the criminal world of Chicago.

Madame Haupt   Ona's midwife. This "enormously fat" woman is unable to save either Ona or her baby.

Freddie Jones   Son of Jurgis' former boss. This drunken playboy provides Jurgis with an unforgettable evening and a $100 bill.

Buck Holloran and Bush Harper   Members of Mike Scully's political machine who work with Jurgis. They make sure that they take care of themselves first.

Ostrinski   A tailor. He introduces the world of socialism from the workingman's perspective.

Tommy Hinds   Jurgis' final boss. This hotelkeeper is one of the organizers of the state Socialist Party, and his hotel is the site of many political discourses.

Lucas   A traveling socialist speaker. Jurgis is one of the guests at a dinner party where this orator debates and defines socialism.

Nicholas Schliemann   A socialist theoretician. He, along with Lucas, serve to state Sinclair's view of socialism. Although Jurgis hears him debate socialism with Lucas, he really exists as a way for Sinclair to talk to readers.

Character Map

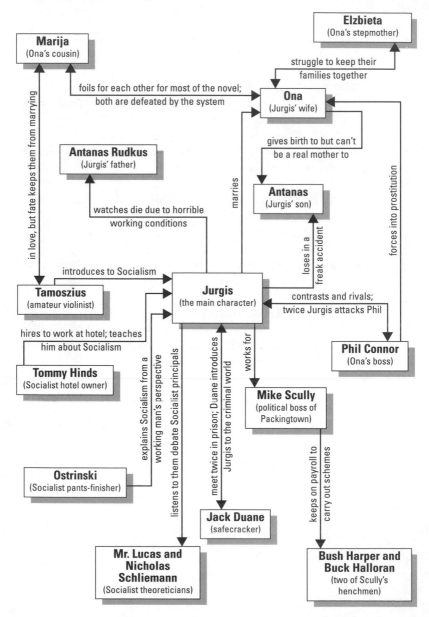

Marija (Ona's cousin)

Elzbieta (Ona's stepmother)

struggle to keep their families together

Ona (Jurgis' wife)

foils for each other for most of the novel; both are defeated by the system

in love, but fate keeps them from marrying

Antanas Rudkus (Jurgis' father)

gives birth to but can't be a real mother to

marries

Antanas (Jurgis' son)

watches die due to horrible working conditions

forces into prostitution

introduces to Socialism

loses in a freak accident

Tamoszius (amateur violinist)

Jurgis (the main character)

contrasts and rivals; twice Jurgis attacks Phil

hires to work at hotel; teaches him about Socialism

works for

Phil Connor (Ona's boss)

Tommy Hinds (Socialist hotel owner)

explains Socialism from a working man's perspective

meet twice in prison; Duane introduces Jurgis to the criminal world

Mike Scully (political boss of Packingtown)

Ostrinski (Socialist pants-finisher)

listens to them debate Socialist principals

keeps on payroll to carry out schemes

Jack Duane (safecracker)

Mr. Lucas and Nicholas Schliemann (Socialist theoreticians)

Bush Harper and Buck Halloran (two of Scully's henchmen)

CRITICAL COMMENTARIES

Chapter 1 16
Chapter 2 20
Chapter 3 22
Chapter 4 24
Chapter 5 26
Chapter 6 28
Chapter 7 30
Chapter 8 32
Chapter 9 34
Chapter 10 36
Chapter 11 38
Chapter 12 40
Chapter 13 41
Chapter 14 43
Chapter 15 45
Chapter 16 47
Chapter 17 48
Chapter 18 50
Chapter 19 51
Chapter 20 53
Chapter 21 55
Chapter 22 57
Chapter 23 58
Chapter 24 59
Chapter 25 61
Chapter 26 63
Chapter 27 65
Chapter 28 67
Chapter 29 69
Chapter 30 71
Chapter 31 73

Chapter 1

Summary

The Jungle begins on the wedding day of two Lithuanian immigrants, Jurgis and Ona, highlighting many of the traditional Lithuanian customs that family members like Marija and Teta Elzbieta attempt to keep alive now that they live in Chicago. Jurgis and Ona have had to wait a long time after immigrating to the United States and settling in Chicago for their wedding to occur due to the economic hardships they've suffered. These hardships are laid out in Chapter 2, as the book continues in a flashback to before the time they met in Lithuania. The flashback continues until Chapter 7 of the book, where the story catches up to the wedding of Jurgis and Ona. Although many people are getting their fill of food and drink, a majority of the guests aren't fulfilling their end of the unwritten agreement to give a gift of money, and the bride and groom don't receive enough funds to start their married life together. In fact, they aren't receiving enough money even to pay for the reception, though, following the Old World tradition, no guest will be turned away. Jurgis, the protagonist, attempts to accept responsibility for this situation by declaring, "I will work harder."

Commentary

Upton Sinclair opens his novel *in media res*—in the middle of the action—capturing the variety of emotions that surround every wedding day. Marija's barking at the carriage driver not only reveals her temperament and provides a glimpse of her strength of character; it also allows Sinclair to provide some history for his characters as well as providing the setting for the entire text. Marija is one of many immigrants who now call Chicago home, and with whom the book is concerned.

Most of the action takes place in Chicago at the turn of the century. The stockyards play a pivotal role, serving as both setting and character. As the setting, the stockyards capture a time and place—the meat packing industry at the turn of the century. The stockyards can be considered a character due to the influence and effect they have on

Jurgis and his family. Sinclair develops the stockyards—through physical description, the comments of other characters, and direct commentary—more than any other character in The Jungle.

At the wedding feast, a variety of attitudes about life in America are revealed. The most important one comes from Dede Antanas (Grandfather Anthony) who "has been only six months in America," yet his toast to the newly married couple is pessimistic, revealing his disillusionment with America.

Sinclair uses information he supplies about one character to reveal important information about many characters. For example, Ona, the bride, is small and dependent. Her physical description prepares readers for the difficulties she faces in Chicago and enables readers to understand why Jurgis feels a need to protect her.

In opposition to Ona is her cousin, Marija, who is strong and concerned about appearances. Marija runs the entire wedding, and her emphasis on doing what is proper and right serves as a dark contrast to the woman she will become. From the onset, readers view Marija as a vigorous woman, a survivor.

Other characters at the wedding serve as glimpses of both the present and the future: The elderly stubbornly cling to Lithuanian customs while the young disregard tradition. References are made to children scavenging the dump for chicken food. The saloonkeepers are cheating the families, and the families begrudgingly accept the swindling because the barmen have connections with the politicians. Some workers are unemployed because of blood poisoning. No workers, not even the bride or groom, are able to take a day off from their jobs. Other couples cannot marry for lack of money. Although the wedding feast is a time for celebration, it is only one day out of a dreary existence for all who live in Packingtown.

Literary Device

Sinclair introduces Jurgis, the main character, almost in an aside. Not much is revealed about the man, although he is described as a "hunted animal." Animal imagery plays a significant part throughout the development of characters and themes in The Jungle, as are the last words of the chapter, "I will work harder." These words characterize Jurgis; however, many times when things are out of his control, so it doesn't matter how hard he works, he still may not succeed.

Stylistically, the narrative structure of *The Jungle* bothers some readers because Sinclair uses an all-knowing narrator. Sinclair used this form for a variety of reasons. First of all, *The Jungle*, like most novels of this time period, was originally published in serial form, and this type of narrative functions well in that particular format: Having a narrative voice outside the story to relate the action makes it easier for readers to follow the installments. Readers who don't appreciate this style do not typically enjoy early (Victorian) novels because the extensive narrative intrusions are bothersome to those who enjoy modern novels. Sinclair also desired to show life as he believed it really existed; therefore, his realistic fiction not only illustrates the real world, it attempts to capture the readers' attention by presenting characters who seemingly have genuine lives separate from the text. The narrator talks about what characters say, think, and do. Most contemporary novels are told from a particular character's point of view, allowing readers some internal insight, which is why many contemporary readers resist novels where a narrator "tells" what happens instead of "showing" the reader what happens.

Other readers are bothered by Sinclair's use of the second person "you." For example, when he discusses the payment of the bar tab, he writes, "You might complain." Sinclair uses "you" in the plural, "you all" form, to connect the reader to both the character and the situation. In addition to shifting from the third to the second person point of view, Sinclair also shifts from past to present tense, and this technique disturbs the unity of time and place while confusing some readers. Most critics concur that the time shifting is a result of hasty writing rather than for any literary purpose.

The problems the family faces at their reception in the New World mirror the problems they encounter in their new lives in America. The focal point of *The Jungle* is the plight of the immigrants. A major part of the problem is the excessive amount of graft and corruption in Packingtown. So many problems exist for the immigrants that the excitement of the wedding changes to trepidation about the next working day—just as their excitement about the New World has changed from optimism to pessimism.

Throughout *The Jungle* Sinclair explores how heredity, environment, and background all shape fate. The lower class is trapped by the very nature of capitalism. Sinclair contrasts Lithuania, where the characters were healthier and happier to where they are now, downtrodden and desperate in the slums of Chicago.

Style & Language

The meaning of foreign words and phrases are revealed through context, providing a sense of authenticity while simultaneously making the immigrants sympathetic to readers. Sinclair needs to have sympathetic characters in order to demonstrate how capitalism destroys them and their families; by presenting capitalism as the problem, he is able to present socialism as the solution. His novel is filled with contrasts; for example, from the onset capitalism is dishonest, a direct contrast to the honest, hard workers. In the first chapter of *The Jungle*, only the slightest hints of Sinclair's agenda are present; however, the predators of capitalism are immediately exposed, as are their prey—the working poor.

Glossary

(Here, and in the following glossaries, difficult and some foreign words and phrases are explained.)

personage   a person of importance or distinction.

veselija   the Lithuanian wedding celebration which includes but is not limited to traditional foods, dances, and behaviors.

viands   food of various kinds; especially, choice dishes.

caper   to skip or jump about in a playful manner.

swain   a young rustic lover.

grandes dames   women, especially older ones, of great dignity or prestige.

quaff   to drink deeply in a hearty or thirsty way.

Faust   the hero of several medieval legends and later literary and operatic works, a philosopher who sells his soul to the devil in exchange for knowledge and power; here, and in several places throughout *The Jungle*, Sinclair inserts literary allusions that are not compatible with the educational level of the character, a stylistic shortcoming.

ponas   Lithuanian word meaning master, gentleman.

brass check   refers to the style of time clock used during this period.

Chapter 2

Summary

The opening of Chapter 2 describes how the foreman for Brown and Company chooses to hire Jurgis, due to his size and strength, and then the narrative continues as a flashback, providing information about how Jurgis and Ona meet and come to America. In Lithuania, both of their families were economically oppressed. After Ona's father died, Jurgis had an opportunity to be with the woman he loved. He takes Ona, his love; Teta Elzbieta, her aunt; Elzbieta's six children; Marija, Ona's cousin; Jonas, Elzbieta's brother; and Jurgis' father, Antenas, to the New World.

For the immigrants, America promised to be the land of opportunity, especially Chicago, where a member of their village had found success. From the onset of their trip, the family was cheated, first by their travel agent, then by officials in New York. After a long journey, and while they were still an hour away, the smells of Packingtown both greeted and offended them. By chance, they meet Jokubus Szedvilas—the man from their village—who runs a delicatessen. He welcomes them to Chicago and sends them to spend the night as boarders for Mrs. Jukniene.

Commentary

Literary Device

The flashback is important for two reasons. First, it provides the exposition of the novel. The exposition is the explanatory information about characters, setting, and prior actions that enables readers to understand the action that follows. Readers get a glimpse of the life Jurgis and Ona left behind in Lithuania and of their difficult journey to Chicago. Sinclair uses a summary narrative here and throughout most of The Jungle. Instead of dramatizing their journey, he tells what happened. The flashback also illustrates a theme of the book: that oppression is not limited to America but rather to any country involved in a competitive economic system.

Literary Device

The sights, sounds, and especially the smells of the factories, which initially repulse Jurgis and his family, serve as a contrast to both the forest they left behind and the city and lifestyle they eventually grow accustomed to. Sinclair foreshadows many of the hardships and difficulties Jurgis and his family endure. Sinclair must detail the bad (assuredly, because very little good did exist) in order to capture the reality of the situation. By doing so, Sinclair uses the Zolaist approach to writing. The French novelist Emile Zola, one of the founders of the literary technique of naturalism, referred to human beings as "human beasts." This points to Sinclair's use of animal imagery throughout The Jungle.

Literary Device

In this chapter, Sinclair makes use of second person to appeal to the reader, and he mentions scavenging the dump for food; however, this time the food is not just for the chickens but also for human consumption. As the novel progresses, Sinclair reveals more and more disturbing and disgusting details, to demonstrate the downside of capitalism.

In spite of gloomy surroundings, Jurgis is hopeful and optimistic at the end of Chapter 2, declaring, "Tomorrow I shall go there and get a job!" Jurgis is a *naïf*, used to illustrate appearance versus reality. A *naïf* is a naïve person who eventually learns the reality and hardships of the world. In the beginning, a naïf is innocent, trusting both people and the socioeconomic system in which he lives; however, as others exploit him, he gradually learns the truth. As Jurgis travels through *The Jungle*, impatience and pessimism gradually replaces his eagerness and optimism.

Glossary

silpnas Lithuanian word meaning weak, faint, delicate.

pall an overspreading covering, as of dark clouds or black smoke, that cloaks or obscures in a gloomy, depressing way.

felicitous used or expressed in a way suitable to the occasion; appropriate.

sordid squalid; depressingly wretched.

Chapter 3

Summary

Szedvilas attempts to find a job for both Antanas and Jonas, but Jurgis refuses his help and is determined to find a job himself. After waiting just half an hour, Jurgis does indeed get a job shoveling guts from a killing floor. Upon hearing Jurgis' news, Szedvilas takes the new arrivals on a tour of Packingtown. First they see the seemingly endless supply of railroads and cattle. Next Szedvilas takes them to a hog factory. Here Jurgis sees the work of the packers—at least what the owners allow the public to see. The technologically advanced pork assembly-line type of killing mechanism enables the industry to "use everything about the hog except the squeal." The dismembering of pigs contrasts with the beef plant Jurgis sees next. Not willing to waste a single portion of the animal, the Beef Trust—the organization of meat industry owners—even uses parts of the animal in the making of fertilizer. Tomorrow, Jurgis becomes a part of the system.

Commentary

Most of this chapter is a *process definition*; that is, it systematically describes the steps of killing and cleaning a hog. The tour Szedvilas provides Jurgis also enables the reader to experience the factories. For many, the mere thought of the killing floors is repulsive, and yet this is just the first of the horrors of Packingtown revealed in the book.

Critics disagree about the success of Sinclair's hog allegory. Some think he is too extreme in his comparison and thus undermines the very point he wants to make. Others find it an extremely fitting way of recognizing the way the system used its own employees to walk to their deaths—killing themselves for the sake of progress, technology, and profits.

At the end of the chapter, Sinclair is openly critical of competition. His narrator blasts the laws of the land that supposedly require competitors, in this case Brown and Durham, to "try to ruin each other under penalty of fine and imprisonment!" This is the first of many anti-capitalistic remarks made throughout *The Jungle*. Unlike the previous allusions to the destructive nature of capitalism, now and subsequently throughout the text, Sinclair openly mentions the problems that he perceives as the direct result of a capitalistic society.

Style & Language

Sinclair uses the word "you," but he now also uses the first person pronoun "our" when referring to "our friends." Three potential explanations for this usage exist. The first is reductive in nature; that is, Sinclair is just a mediocre author who makes an error in consistency and voice. Although he is not currently as esteemed as a few of his peers, this is not a satisfying explanation. A different interpretation suggests this as another example of Sinclair's attempt to gain sympathy for the family. Using "our" encourages readers to accept Jurgis and his family as members of their own families. A final suggestion is that Sinclair uses the rhetoric of the socialist movement—where everyone is a "comrade"—in an indirect manner, familiarizing readers with the notion of unity and oneness before directly mentioning socialism. Critics can debate Sinclair's style and use of language, but they cannot debate the fact that Sinclair presents Jurgis as "guileless" and "ignorant of the nature of business." At this point in time, Jurgis has complete faith in the American dream.

Glossary

colloquy   a conversation, especially a formal discussion.

menagerie   a collection of wild or strange animals kept in cages or enclosures for exhibition.

drover   a person who herds droves of animals, especially to market.

parley   a talk or conference for the purpose of discussing a specific matter.

ptomaines   substances, some of which are poisonous, formed in decaying animal matter.

isinglass   a form of gelatin made from the internal membranes of fish bladders: used as a clarifying agent and adhesive.

pepsin   an extract of gastric juice enzymes from the stomachs of calves, pigs, etc., formerly used as a digestive aid.

albumen   water-soluble protein.

Chapter 4

Summary

Jurgis reports for work but does not know how to enter the plant. Hours later, once inside, he sweeps waste parts into the vat below the killing floors. The work is hard but Jurgis is glad to be working. Jonas is granted an interview, and Marija finds a job; Jurgis decides Ona and Elzbieta will not have to work. Things are tough but will seemingly be all right.

Then Jurgis receives a flyer advertising a house for sale. The family is lured by the flyer's claim that paying rent is a waste of money, and they desire a house of their own. Although the house they see is not exactly what they expected, the agent soon convinces them of its merits, and a lengthy debate ensues. Eventually, Jurgis makes the decision to buy it.

Jurgis is unable to complete the transaction because he cannot leave his job at the killing floor, so Ona and Teta Elzbieta must meet with the sales agent instead. Szedvilas offers what little assistance he can. Some confusion about the wording of the contract exists, but Elzbieta proceeds with the transaction. Afterwards, when Jurgis hears of the potential complication, he becomes enraged and storms out, threatening to kill the agent. Only after consulting another lawyer is Jurgis somewhat appeased.

Commentary

Jurgis has a job and doesn't understand why others aren't equally satisfied with just being able to work. He is able to get his first job rather easily because of his size and strength (however, when he loses these attributes, he has a hard time finding a job).

Sinclair continues to contrast Marija with Ona. Marija is a go-getter who is able to find a job, while Ona stays home with the children. Marija gets her job, however, only through the misfortune of another. This is the first of many examples of the exploitative capitalistic system that works young children and ignores the injured and the elderly.

Literary
Device

With many family members working, having found jobs rather easily, it is understandable that the allure of owning a house and creating a home captures the fancy of the family. However, both the house and Jurgis' wrath foreshadow future problems. The house symbolizes the American dream. But just as their dwelling is not really what it is presented as being, so too is the American dream false. Soon the house becomes an economic burden, forcing children to drop out of school in order to pay expenses. The dream becomes a nightmare as their lives become a living hell.

Glossary

besom   a broom, especially one made of twigs tied to a handle.

volubility   an ability or tendency to talk much and easily.

Chapter 5

Summary

Almost immediately, expenses for the house consume all the family's money. Jurgis still cannot understand why many of the men hate their work, and he has his first encounter with the union, which, at this point, he has no use for.

Throughout the chapter, Antanas is still job hunting. The only opportunity he has to work entails losing 33% of his earnings weekly—payment to the man who found the job for him—and although this is outrageous, he accepts. Once hired, Antanas is forced to partake in the unethical and illegal activities of the meatpacking industry. Jurgis also witnesses and partakes in improper meat-production activities. During this time he comes to realize those who laughed at his faith in America "might be right."

Marija's job is also the result of an unethical practice: She takes the place of a sick woman who had worked at the same job for 15 years. The forelady did not care that the previous employee had worked the job for so long; she only knew that she missed one day of work.

Commentary

The exposure to the surface-level graft and corruption serves as the beginning of Jurgis' disillusionment. Initially he has no interest in the union: Jurgis has a job and is a hard worker. He is used to fending for himself and does not view joining the union as an investment; rather, it is a waste of money. Later on Jurgis' opinion changes.

All is not what it seems—in the area of home ownership as well as employment—and both are examples of foreshadowing. Initially Jurgis is shocked and dismayed at the illegal and unethical practices in his workplace. In a couple of short years, he learns that the only way he can find economic security within the system is by abusing it.

Although Sinclair's authorial intention in *The Jungle* is to illustrate the plight of the immigrants and the folly of capitalism, his novel is remembered more for illuminating the abuses in the meatpacking industry. In this chapter he describes the first of many illegal and immoral activities. Throughout *The Jungle* Sinclair attempts to create a realistic portrayal of life in Packingtown, and for the most part he succeeds. The problem is that it is not easy for readers to discern fact from fiction. Sinclair exercises poetic license in his narrative, yet many readers readily accept his fiction as the literal truth.

Glossary

laissez faire   the policy of letting the owners of industry and business fix the rules of competition, the conditions of labor, etc., as they please, without governmental regulation or control.

Malthus   Thomas Malthus (1766–1834); an English economist who held the theory that the world population tends to increase faster than the food supply with inevitable disastrous results unless natural restriction, such as war, famine, and disease reduce the population or the increase is checked by moral restraint.

knave   a dishonest, deceitful person; a tricky rascal.

Chapter 6

Summary

From an old Lithuanian widow, Grandmother Majauszkiene, Jurgis and his family learn that their house is not brand new; in fact, it is fifteen years old. Jurgis is the fifth person to attempt to pay for this particular house, paying a price that is already three times the cost to build it. Majauszkiene also mentions paying interest on the mortgage; this is news to Jurgis, who again vows to work harder. Now Ona and Stanislovas, one of Elzbieta's children, must seek employment. Ona pays $10 to get a job at Brown's, and Stanislovas lies about his age, with help from the priest, and lands a job tending a lard machine. With another disaster seemingly averted, Jurgis and Ona once again begin to discuss plans for their wedding.

Commentary

Although Chapter 6 begins and ends with mention of the love between Jurgis and Ona, the pages in between show how the public manifestation of their love—their wedding—must be postponed as bills and adversity dominate their lives.

Literary Device

In the middle of their misfortune, Jurgis and Ona meet Grandmother Majauszkiene. As a character, Grandmother Majauszkiene serves two major purposes. The first deals with the influx of immigrants. Having worked hard enough and long enough to purchase her house, she has lived in the neighborhood long enough to see many families come and go, attempting unsuccessfully to make timely house payments. Tragedy strikes each family and ethnic group—the Germans, the Irish, the Bohemians, and the Poles—but the builders, who represent industry, don't care about the struggles of working people. Grandmother Majauszkiene is also the first socialist Jurgis encounters. Not much is made of her political affiliation; in fact it is referred to as a "strange thing." It is strange only because it is different, and it isn't talked about because Jurgis is not yet in a position to be willing to listen to and appreciate the party's message.

Theme

The dependence on money is of paramount importance from this chapter until the end of the book. Constantly Jurgis works harder and harder, only to find himself further and further in debt. The house, due to the added and hidden expenses, ends up costing much more than it initially appears to. The false sense of security that buying the house suggests parallels the false sense of security immigrants have when coming to America. Immigrants are seduced by promises of riches and success and are willing to work extremely hard to turn their dreams into reality; but Sinclair argues that the system isn't designed to promote success. In fact, as more and more youths are forced to join the labor force in order to help keep their families alive; the very American dream that lured immigrant families to America destroys those families.

Glossary

lose all caste   to lose social status or position.

consumption   a disease causing the wasting away of the body, especially, formerly, tuberculosis of the lungs.

Chapter 7

Summary

Summer passes into fall, and Jurgis and Ona are finally able to marry. The narrative flashback has now reached the time of the opening chapter. Unfortunately for the newlyweds, life is still tough and seemingly only getting tougher. Ona seems to be constantly sick, as are Elzbieta's children. And Dede Antanas develops both a dreadful cough and sores, which eventually lead to his death. Jurgis is too poor to pay for a proper burial.

The winter takes its toll on everyone in Packingtown. A young boy who works with Stanislovas loses his ears to frostbite, and Stanislovas becomes deathly afraid of venturing out in the cold. Jurgis must now carry the boy to work. Most men turn to alcohol in order to escape from the harsh realities of their jobs and the weather; Jurgis does not out of respect for Ona. This winter, no one in Packingtown is living; they are all slowly dying.

Commentary

Ironically, the event which should symbolize love and happiness—the wedding—ends up being the event that pushes the couple further into debt, adding more stress and frustration to their already harried lives. As Jurgis reflects about what has happened to him, he begins to lose some of his innocence.

Theme

Chapter 7 illustrates Charles Darwin's theory of survival of the fittest. All immigrants are facing harsh conditions; only the strong survive. Dede Antanas is old and weak and subsequently dies. Stanislovas, representing the young, doesn't suffer a physical death but does suffer an emotional death. Literally scared to death of the weather, Jurgis must physically force him to go to work. It is no wonder that the old and young—who should not even be working in the first place—are the first to die: They are not the strongest.

Literary
Device

The weakest die first, and just like dead branches on a tree, are the first to fall to the ground. Sinclair continues his jungle comparison by discussing people in terms of branches: Soon they are shaken from the tree. This tree is also used as an analogy for Lithuania. Unwittingly, Jurgis and his family moved from one jungle into another. In opposition to those who die are those who survive, and survival in this jungle, as foreshadowed in this chapter, means drinking and prostitution. This survival, though, is only a physical one, for the spirit is eventually destroyed. The body is also destroyed—either through alcohol, injury, or disease.

Glossary

pathos   the quality in something experienced or observed which arouses feelings of pity, sorrow, sympathy, or compassion.

vermin   various insects, bugs, or small animals regarded as pests because they are destructive or disease-carrying, such as flies, lice, rats, or weasels.

saltpeter   potassium nitrate, which is a colorless, crystalline compound used in fertilizers, gunpowder, and preservatives, etc.

hack   a carriage or coach for hire.

grippe   influenza.

Chapter 8

Summary

Once again, Jurgis is approached about joining the union, and now that he recognizes and understands many of the abuses inherent in the system, he agrees to join. He also convinces the other members of his family to join, and their faith in their well being is now restored. Jurgis begins to attend union meetings and encourages others to join. The union becomes his religion, and the new convert zealously attempts to show others the light.

Commentary

A recurring motif in *The Jungle*—that in the real world love places second to economics—dominates this chapter. In addition to the difficulties that Jurgis and Ona experience, come the problems with Marija and Tamoszius' relationship. During the months following the wedding, Marija and Tamoszius Kuszleika develop a close relationship, and they plan to marry in the springtime. Then, without notice, the canning factory Marija work in shuts down. The relationship again illustrates Marija's strength, but strength of character, as seen with Jurgis, is not always enough.

This seasonal shortage of work also affects Jurgis, who receives fewer hours and subsequently less pay. Although he must still report to work at 7:00 a.m., sometimes work does not start until the late afternoon, and men receive wages only for actual hours worked. Jurgis now sides with organized labor against the establishment. His passion for the union foreshadows the zeal he develops for socialism. Jurgis now begins his long fight against the unfair practices of management; his life is that of a war—the worker versus the industry.

Glossary

eloquent   vividly expressive.

impropriety   improper action or behavior.

tacit   not expressed or declared openly, but implied or understood.

skylarking   playing about boisterously.

impunity   freedom or exemption from punishment, penalty, or harm.

Chapter 9

Summary

His union involvement leads Jurgis to learn English and to discover politics. Mike Scully is the democratic boss of Packingtown. Scully and his men encourage immigrants like Jurgis to become naturalized citizens and to vote in the local elections. Jurgis and others are shown how to vote and are paid to vote the democratic ticket. Through Scully and the elected politicians, Jurgis learns of the graft and corruption running rampant in Packingtown, which is far greater than the scams he has encountered at the factory. From his co-workers Jurgis hears about some of the most outlandish practices, and with his own eyes he observes the variety of afflictions particular to specific tradesmen. The worst scenario takes place at the fertilizer plant—a place no visitor ever sees because of the stench of the place and its workers—where occasionally a worker falls in and it is impossible to fish him out, so he becomes part of the finished product.

Commentary

Style & Language

Chapter 9 serves primarily as Sinclair's muckraker chapter. A *muckraker* searches for and publicizes corruption by public officials and businesses. The problem with muckrakers, though, is that they publicize both real and alleged corruption. The abuses described in this chapter are what gives *The Jungle* its notoriety; however, the accuracy of Sinclair's reporting is definitely in question.

Sinclair was not writing an exposé of the meatpacking industry. Rather, he was describing the plight of the immigrants. He has taken some incidents of abuses and problems, added a bit of poetic license, and fictionalized the accounts of what he knew was going on. As noted, Sinclair admitted that "I aimed at the public's heart, and by accident I hit it in the stomach." Sinclair's bias is best illustrated when he refers to factories in Packingtown as the "spoiled meat industry."

Citing the U.S. Rules and Regulations is a journalistic technique Sinclair uses that detracts from the novel. The citation, in the form of a footnote, adds nothing to the development of the plot, characters, or themes; rather, it exists as a means for something to rail against. Sinclair uses this chapter to find fault with regulations and procedures. His famous controversial example of the man falling into the vat and becoming fertilizer is presented as realistic when in all probability it is very far-fetched. Many people reading *The Jungle*, however, may accept this anecdote as a common occurrence and may remember the novel as a meatpacking industry exposé rather than as a novel about the plight of immigrants.

An important thematic element resonates throughout Chapter 9: The rich own everything and that's just the way of the world. This situation existed in Lithuania and is demonstrated very clearly in Chicago. Another reality of America is the political system, depicted as two parties of elected grafters; politics is as corrupt as the meatpacking industry.

Glossary

leviathan   something huge or very powerful.

scow   large flat-bottomed boat with square ends, used for carrying coal, sand, etc., and often towed by a tug.

injunction   writ or order from a court prohibiting a person or group from carrying out a given action.

trichinae   very small nematode worms found in insufficiently cooked pork that cause trichinosis, which is a disease characterized by fever, nausea, diarrhea, and muscular pains.

Dante   born Durante Alighieri (1265–1321), Italian poet famous for *The Divine Comedy* where he describes the stages of hell.

Zola   Émile Zola (1840–1902); French novelist who founded the writing style of naturalism (also called Zolaism) emphasizing the harsh realities of the world.

alchemist   person who practices alchemy, a seemingly miraculous power or process of changing a thing into something better.

rancid   having the bad smell or taste of stale fats or oils; spoiled.

Chapter 10

Summary

Each season brings a new catastrophe, forcing Jurgis and his family to fight just to barely survive. In the spring they learn that in addition to the mortgage and the taxes, they have to pay insurance on their property. The messy spring rain gives way to the stifling summer heat. Marija gets her job back when the factory re-opens, only to lose it due to her union activity. Ona is pregnant, so it is imperative for Marija to find a new job. She reluctantly accepts work as a beef trimmer, a job she would have refused earlier. Ona discovers that her boss operates a brothel downtown and many decent girls lose their positions at the factory to prostitutes. Jurgis insists on having a male doctor instead of a midwife when Ona gives birth to their son, who is named Antanas—after the child's grandfather, Dede Antanas. Jurgis is unable to see much of his son because of the long hours he works, and Ona must return to work after missing only a week, in order not to lose her position. Ona, who has never been very strong or healthy, never fully recovers from this experience and suffers for the rest of her days with the same ailments that affect most of the factory women, for all women return to work too quickly after giving birth to fully recover.

Commentary

Style & Language

Chapter 10 reads as a case history of abuse. Sinclair provides neither action nor dialogue. Life continues to be extremely difficult, but Jurgis can do nothing to change this. The one bright spot in Jurgis' life is the birth of his son.

Marija lands a job as beef trimmer, making half the amount of the man she replaces. Her character, possessing the "muscles of a man," continues to contrast with Ona, a weak woman who grows weaker after the birth of her son. Ona's weakened condition continues throughout the remainder of the book, foreshadowing her untimely death.

Forced to return to work one week after giving birth, Ona is not able to be a mother to her child. This illustrates the destructive force capitalism is on the family unit. Because he must work long hours on the killing floor, Jurgis is unable to be a father to his child. In fact, he seldom sees little Antanas. According to Sinclair, the very nature of capitalism threatens the integrity of the family.

Sinclair also uses a seemingly throwaway line, "she [Ona] did not tell half of her story at home" to foreshadow the fate not only of Ona but of Marija—their forced prostitution. Another important, naturalistic theme states that a technological society drives women to prostitution. Both strong and weak women eventually turn to the oldest profession—satisfying the carnal whims of men—in order to make the money necessary to keep their families together. Women do not turn to prostitution because they want to, but because they're forced to.

Glossary

bog   wet spongy ground, characterized by decaying mosses that form peat; a small marsh or swamp.

purgatory   a state or place in which, in Roman Catholicism and other Christian doctrine, those who have died in the grace of God expiate their sins by suffering.

furies   in Greek and Roman mythology, the three terrible female spirits with snaky hair who punish the doers of unavenged crimes.

bawdyhouse   a house of prostitution.

Chapter 11

Summary

Although Jurgis is working harder than ever, the process of "speeding up," the hiring of more workers, and a reduction in wages earn him a net loss income. At this time Jurgis learns that all the packers, a term used to refer to the owners and management, conspire together in something known as the Beef Trust.

Marija cares little for this and worries only about herself. She opens a savings account, but is extremely leery of the entire banking system. Panic and an ensuing bank run causes her to miss two days of work to withdraw her money. The run ends up having nothing to do with the bank.

Before they know it, winter has returned again, and the family feels utterly unprepared. Jurgis takes control of the situation as best he can, escorting Ona and carrying Stanislovas to work. Unfortunately, Jurgis sprains his ankle and misses three weeks of work. During this time Ona, unbeknownst to Jurgis, must borrow from their meager savings in order to survive. The only solace Jurgis finds during this difficult time is spending time with his son.

Commentary

Theme

Two important themes dominate Chapter 11. The first states that accidents determine fate. Through no fault of his own, Jurgis is out of work for three weeks. It is an accident that he sprains his ankle, but nonetheless, his entire family suffers for it. One financial crisis follows another, all independent of each other and each seemingly more calamitous than the previous one. A related theme demonstrates that a willingness to work is not always enough. From the onset, Jurgis' motto has been "I will work harder." He has been working harder and harder, but realizing his goals less and less. The corrupt nature of the meatpacking industry stacks the deck against him and all hard workers, for the only ones reaping the benefits of increased work levels are the owners.

A comparison to Lithuania in this chapter is in the food they eat: In the forest, they ate real sausage; here they ingest imitation filler. Once again, the old cliché about "the grass is always greener" comes true. Jurgis and his family did not recognize the advantages and benefits of what they had in Lithuania.

As the months pass by and election time rolls around, Jurgis realizes that selling his vote to the democrats is unethical, but he does it anyway. His attitude is not one of indifference but rather of survival. It really does not matter whether he sells his vote or not, because the democrats will win. But if this opportunity presents a chance for Jurgis to help his family, the ends justify the means. When ethics battles economics, economics wins every time.

Glossary

superfluity   a quantity or number beyond what is needed.

inexorably   relentlessly; unalterable.

Prometheus   in Greek mythology, a Titan who steals fire from heaven for the benefit of mankind. To punish him, Zeus chains him to a rock where a vulture comes each day to eat his liver, which grows back each night.

Chapter 12

Summary

Jurgis attempts to return to work, but the pain of a pulled tendon is unbearable. Jurgis is unable to work for two more months. During this time a major snowstorm strikes, preventing Ona and Stanislovas from getting to work. Attempting to do so, Stanislovas freezes his hands, permanently ruining the joints in several fingers. From this point on, Jurgis must beat the boy in order to get him to go to work.

In the spring, Jonas suddenly disappears. The loss of his income convinces Jurgis that two more of Elzbieta's sons must quit school and go to work selling newspapers. Ona is deteriorating both physically and emotionally, but Jurgis is unable to recognize this or respond to her need for reassurance of his love for her.

When Jurgis is finally strong enough to work again, he no longer has a position to return to so he joins the ranks of the unemployed. Now, however, he is no longer a strapping young man and isn't as employable.

Commentary

Theme

Chapter 12 illustrates that cheating exists at all levels of business, from the owners and workers in the big companies to the young boys selling papers. Capitalism and cheating exist hand in hand.

Jonas' disappearance can be accounted for in one of two ways. He may be a victim of an industrial accident and subsequent cover-up, or he may, in all likelihood, have just left. In Packingtown, having a family is a curse, not a blessing, and Jonas can find more success on his own, so it is more quite possible that Jonas abandoned his family.

In addition to having been injured on the job, Jurgis is no longer the brawny young man he once was, and the industry that weakened and practically destroyed him no longer wants him. Jurgis searches in vain for any sort of employment, but he is no longer a viable candidate.

Glossary

penury lack of money, property, or necessities; extreme poverty.

Chapter 13

Summary

While Jurgis searches for work, another tragedy strikes the family: Kristoforas, Elzbieta's youngest child, dies. She begs from the neighbors in order to have enough money for a funeral. Unable to find work anywhere else, Jurgis applies for and accepts a job at the fertilizer factory. From the moment he begins shoveling fertilizer into carts, Jurgis is covered with dust and begins suffering from headaches and dizziness. And now he smells horribly. But at least he has a job. During the summer, Elzbieta's sons take up disturbing habits—swearing, smoking, gambling, and not coming home—and in order to break them of these habits, Elzbieta herself goes to work, enabling her sons to return to school. If they attend school, then they will not be out on the streets. She ends up finding work in a sausage house, twisting sausage links.

Commentary

Theme

Continuing his elaboration of survival of the fittest, Sinclair emphasizes survival techniques throughout Chapter 13. After weeks of frustration, Jurgis finally agrees to seek employment at the worst possible site—the fertilizer plant. Jurgis is out of options and accepts the job, and even though it makes him physically ill, he keeps the job. He is determined to earn a living and support his family, no matter the cost to him as an individual. Fertilizer invades his clothes as the stench invades his person, and Jurgis is forced to live with his choice every moment of every day.

Character Insight

Like Jurgis, Elzbieta does something she does not want to do: She gets a job. She does this in order to allow her children to attend school. Jurgis and Elzbieta represent the old-world work ethic, where parents endure all sorts of hardships for the sake of their children, working hard and sacrificing with the hope that their children will have a better life. Elzbieta and the other workers at the sausage plant are compared to animals in cages: When visitors tour the plant, they're encouraged to focus on the machines and not the people, which is what the tourists do. This not-too-subtle comment emphasizes the value of technology while simultaneously devaluing humans, another complaint directed towards capitalism.

Literary Device

When Kristoforas dies, Marija loans Elzbieta some money for funeral expenses. This foreshadows the fact that one day the entire family will depend on Marija's income for survival, especially at a time when Jurgis is either unwilling or unable to provide for their basic wants and needs.

Glossary

obdurate   not easily moved to pity or sympathy; hardhearted.

charnel   a building or place where corpses or bones are deposited.

savant   a learned person; eminent scholar.

ptarmigan   a brownish bird with feathered legs and feet, usually having white plumage in the winter.

prestidigitator   an expert at sleight of hand.

Chapter 14

Summary

The variety of jobs that the various members of Jurgis' family work in Packingtown enables them to experience firsthand the various "Packingtown swindles." Jurgis turns to alcohol to deal with his frustrations and sense of defeat. He does not succumb to the temptation all at once, but rather he gradually submits to its false promises of escape. While Jurgis starts to drink, Ona's deterioration accelerates. She has fits of hysteria and nervousness that Jurgis cannot understand and Elzbieta cannot explain. Though she blames it on another pregnancy, Jurgis thinks it is something more than that.

Commentary

In Sinclair's most graphic example of business abuse—the sweeping of poison, rats, and rat dung into the food vat—he is most likely employing a form of *hyperbole*, an extended exaggeration to make a point. Admittedly, abuses within the system existed, many conditions were unsanitary, and workers were apathetic; but Sinclair once again employs literary license to gain support for his characters and his political ideology.

As is the standard of naturalistic fiction, the stock characters in *The Jungle* are driven to drink or prostitution. In an industrialized society, no other options exist. Curiously, Jurgis blames marriage and sex for his woes and not the owners as he gradually begins to drink, succumbing to the temptations of alcohol. Alcohol becomes the solution for many of his problems for some time to come. Ona's prostitution is only foreshadowed, but its effects are evident. She becomes hysterical and breaks down often and is compared to a wounded animal. And the way of life in the jungle is that the wounded are destroyed and devoured.

Glossary

torpor dullness; apathy.

specter any object of fear or dread.

prodigy a person, thing, or act so extraordinary as to inspire wonder.

conjurer magician.

Chapter 15

Summary

Around Thanksgiving, Ona doesn't return home one night after work. Jurgis goes to her factory the next morning to wait for her. When she arrives, Ona explains that she couldn't make it home because of the storm and spent the night with a friend. A month later Ona again does not return home, but this time Jurgis is not concerned until he stops by her friend's house only to find that Ona did not spend the night there nor had she ever done so.

Her fellow employees know the truth but refuse to reveal it to Jurgis. By chance he notices Ona on a streetcar and follows her home. He demands to know the truth about her whereabouts, and Ona reveals to Jurgis that she has been to her forelady's house. It takes Jurgis a moment to realize exactly what this means. When he finally understands, he finds out that Connor, one of her bosses, has been taking her downtown, using threats against her family as leverage to make Ona comply with his wishes.

Jurgis storms from the house enraged, and rushes to the plant. There he finds Connor and attacks him, attempting to strangle him. Many men are needed to pull Jurgis off of Connor, and eventually Jurgis is taken to the company police station to await a patrol wagon.

Commentary

Character Insight

Chapter 15 provides readers with the first and only meaningful exchange between Jurgis and Ona. Jurgis, in a rage, confronts his wife about her deceptions and lies. Although the scene borders on melodrama, readers can empathize, experiencing both Jurgis' rage and Ona's fears. Unwittingly, Jurgis is as cruel to Ona as Connor had been. Ona, the weaker one, again submits to the will of anyone who is stronger than she is.

As soon as Ona reveals that the unrelenting economic pressure forced her into prostitution, Jurgis becomes unglued. His attack on Connor is both understandable and unwise. Physically, Connor is no match for

Jurgis, but in Packingtown, power depends more on connections and money than it does on brute strength.

Theme

This entire incident illustrates the connection between coincidence, chance, and fate. Connor victimizes Ona from the onset of her employment. Any number of possibilities could have prevented the truth from being revealed: Ona might have been able to make it home either night, or Jurgis might not have attempted to find her, or Connor may have grown tired of her. Regardless of the "what ifs" and "could have beens," the truth did come out, with devastating results. This scene demonstrates that in the jungle of Packingtown, characters are not only prey for beasts, they are bestial themselves. Jurgis' attack on Connor is a demonstration of his most animalistic behavior yet.

Glossary

bullocks   young bulls.

rife   abundant.

tempest   a violent storm with high winds.

Chapter 16

Summary

At the police station Jurgis is booked on charges of assault and battery. After his satisfaction at taking revenge on Connor subsides, Jurgis begins to worry about Ona and the family. He is convinced they will lose the house. Incarcerated on Christmas Eve, Jurgis hears the church bells and curses the injustice and insanity of American society.

Commentary

Readers sympathize with Jurgis and understand his attack on Connor, but the courts do not. As readers side with Jurgis, it is easier for them to agree with his conclusion that justice is a lie and does not exist. Capitalism not only adversely affects the workers, its evil infiltrates the seemingly unbiased judicial system. In reality, the courts are just as corrupt as industry is.

Character Insight

While in jail, Jurgis determines that society is his enemy. His conclusions mark the beginning of a new Jurgis. He no longer is the naïve young immigrant who arrived ready to work, eager to fulfill the American dream. The reference at the end of the chapter to an Oscar Wilde poem is clearly from Sinclair's and not Jurgis' experience. Although the sentiment matches the scenario, the literary allusion is inappropriate, because Jurgis, an uneducated immigrant, would have no knowledge of Wilde.

Glossary

melee   a noisy, confused fight or hand-to-hand struggle among a number of people.

glutted   fed to excess.

fetid   having a bad smell, as of decay.

clangor   a continued clanging.

outlawry   disregard or defiance of the law.

Chapter 17

Summary

In the morning, Jack Duane joins Jurgis in the cell. Duane's attitude about the necessary war against society appeals to Jurgis, who is in the beginning of his rebellious stage. Jurgis' trial is a farce, as the judge readily believes Connor's false testimony and sentences Jurgis to 30 days in prison. While there, Stanislovas visits Jurgis, begging for money and telling Jurgis of the continued troubles affecting the family.

Commentary

Jurgis' sham of a trial should surprise no one. The judge is bought and sold like any other tangible good, so even though Connor is the guilty predator, the victim is penalized. The judge does not care that his ruling may force Jurgis' family into starvation.

Jurgis' family suffers a variety of problems during his incarceration marking the beginning of the end. Now all able-bodied children are forced to work, which is precisely what Jurgis and Elzbieta wanted to avoid. Marija becomes the latest worker to sustain an on-the-job injury, which, of course, is not the responsibility of her employer. Yet again, laborers suffer permanent damage as a result of their employment; they are butchered in a manner similar to the other animals in Packingtown. In Packingtown, capitalism is as destructive as the weather and disease.

The introduction of Jack Duane is important as Jurgis begins to enter a new stage in his life. Jurgis' relationship with Duane illustrates how circumstances can force a man into a life of crime. Trying to be a law-abiding, hard-working citizen does Jurgis little good. For his family's sake, Jurgis demonstrates hard work, self-reliance, and values, but when he loses his family, he loses all desire to do the "right" thing.

Glossary

the deuce   the devil; a mild oath or exclamation of annoyance, surprise, or frustration.

freebooter   a plunderer.

bigamist   a person who marries a second time while a previous marriage is still legally in effect.

confidence men   swindlers who try to gain the confidence of victims in order to defraud.

imprecation   a curse.

Black Maria   a patrol wagon.

Chapter 18

Summary

After serving additional time in prison to cover the court costs, Jurgis is released. He returns to his house to find it painted and someone else living there.

An Irishwoman tells him that she recently bought the house. Grandmother Majauszkiene tells Jurgis that his family has returned to the Widow Jukniene's. He races there, finding many women huddled in the kitchen, and is assailed by Ona's screams. Marija explains that her baby has come early and they have no money for a midwife. The women together scrounge up their money, give it to Jurgis, and tell him to search for someone.

Commentary

Jurgis and his family are just one of many in the vicious cycle of abuse which comprises life in Packingtown. Chapter 18 exists mostly to bridge one part of Jurgis' life to the next. Walking the wrong way after being released from prison illustrates the fact that Jurgis is directionless and clueless, yet still does not know to whom he should listen.

Arriving at his house, he finds that what he considered his own is, in reality, not his. Another family has been swindled, just as Jurgis had been. Both his house and his family are gone. Losing his house not only symbolizes the lost American dream, it foreshadows Jurgis' loss of Ona.

When he arrives to find Ona having an early and difficult delivery, readers know that this birth will not be a happy occasion and that Ona will probably die.

Glossary

vitals organs necessary for human life, such as the heart, brain, and lungs, etc.

Chapter 19

Summary

Jurgis' search for a midwife leads him to Madame Haupt, who is reluctant to help because Jurgis has no money to pay. After much debate and Jurgis' leaving in frustration and anger, she agrees to help.

The women again send Jurgis from the house. When he returns, he finds that the baby is dead and Ona is dying. Jurgis rushes to her; she opens her eyes for one brief instant of recognition and dies. He remains numb and shocked until Kotrina arrives home from selling papers. He takes her money and announces that he's going to get drunk.

Commentary

Style & Language

Sinclair provides an excellent description of life in the slums as Jurgis searches for help and, after finally finding some, is dismissed from the scene. The death of Ona is the first of two central turning points in Jurgis' life (the other being the death of his first son later in the book). He was supposed to have been taking care of her, but was unable to do so.

This entire chapter is a series of losses—Jurgis loses his way, his house, and his wife. And all that he has lost has been the fault of the capitalistic society in which he lives. The same society has to depend on the Madame Haupts of the world.

Literary Device

Madame Haupt, an enormously overweight and dirty woman, is one of the few minor characters who are realistically portrayed. Sinclair spends little time developing other minor characters, and as a result, most of them are stereotypes. She, however, is a multi-dimensional character who embodies life in Packingtown: She is the poor man's doctor, the necessary evil.

Glossary

wrapper   a loose garment wrapped around the body; especially, a woman's dressing gown.

wienerwurst   a smoked sausage of beef or beef and pork, etc., enclosed in a membranous casing and made in cylindrical links a few inches long.

lager   a type of beer stored at a low temperature for aging after it has been brewed.

vista   a comprehensive mental view of a series of remembered or anticipated events.

haggard   having a wild, wasted, worn look, as from sleeplessness, grief, or illness.

Chapter 20

Summary

Unable to remain drunk very long on the pittance he has, Jurgis returns to the widow's to find out that Elzbieta has begged enough money to pay for a funeral mass for Ona. Elzbieta uses baby Antanas as leverage as she encourages Jurgis to find a job, but he is refused a job even at the fertilizer plant. Finally he is offered a job, but when he reports for work, the boss tells him that he cannot use him. Jurgis is blacklisted.

After weeks of unemployment, a chance meeting with a former union associate leads Jurgis to a job in the harvester works. Jurgis is heartened by his new job and begins to make plans for the future, only to be laid off ten days later.

Commentary

With Ona's death, the only thing Jurgis lives for is his son, Antanas. True to his character, Jurgis diligently looks for gainful employment. Recognizing his responsibilities as a father, he even returns to the fertilizer plant, but to no avail. More potential workers exist in Packingtown than do jobs; therefore, packers have the ability to blacklist perceived troublemakers. This is another way the owners exercise power over the laborers.

Getting a job outside the city seems to be an ideal situation, because working conditions are better there. Working as a harvester seems better than working in a factory. But work as a harvester is seasonal. When Jurgis is laid off, he realizes he is still at the whim of a capitalistic system that does not care for its employees, only its profits.

Glossary

cur   a dog of mixed breed; a mongrel.

angleworm   an earthworm: so called because it is used for fishing bait.

treason   betrayal of trust or faith.

blacklist   a list of persons who have been censured and who are being discriminated against or refused employment.

valise   a piece of hand luggage.

philanthropist   a person, especially a wealthy one, who is interested in the general human welfare, especially as shown in large-scale gifts to charities.

monopoly   exclusive control of a commodity or service in a given market, or control that makes possible the fixing of prices and the virtual elimination of free competition.

Chapter 21

Summary

Jurgis spends days away from home, looking for work, fighting to stay alive. A chance meeting between Elzbieta's son and a settlement worker provides Jurgis with a letter to the superintendent of a steel mill. Because the mill is far away, Jurgis sleeps at a lodging house during the week, returning to Packingtown on the weekends. An accident at the mill forces Jurgis to miss some work but enables him to spend some time with his son. Marija and Elzbieta are both finally working. It is springtime but Jurgis is already preparing for the next winter. One Saturday, after a heavy rain, Jurgis returns home to discover that Antanas has drowned.

Commentary

Theme

Antanas' death is the second central turning point in *The Jungle*. Just when Jurgis' life appears to be back on track, just when he begins to have hope for the future, fate transforms his dreams into nightmares. Antanas is another character who dies, another victim of fate.

The settlement worker introduced in Chapter 21 represents a reversal of sexual politics—for the first time, a female controls a man based on sex and economics. Her interference, although doing nothing to help the unsafe conditions in the plant, does result in a job for Jurgis. This is the complete opposite of the abusive sexual politics that Connor exercised. Although she is the first woman to exhibit a position of power, the results are still negative. Although she enables Jurgis to find a job, the job keeps him from his family; therefore, he is unable to protect his son.

Literary Device

In fitting literary irony, Sinclair places the death of Antanas during springtime—typically the season of new life and rebirth—and just as Jurgis begins to have a sense of new life and a new beginning, it is literally drowned.

Glossary

settlement   an institution in a depressed and congested neighborhood offering social services and educational and recreational activities.

naïvely   in an unaffectedly, or sometimes foolishly, simple manner; artlessly.

catechism   a formal series of questions; close questioning.

billet   a long, rectangular or cylindrical unfinished bar of iron or steel, usually smaller than 36 inches.

incandescent   very bright; shining brilliantly.

ingot   a mass of metal cast into a bar or other convenient shape.

Chapter 22

Summary

In shock over his son's accidental drowning, Jurgis walks away and impulsively climbs aboard a freight train. Jurgis tries to think only of himself as the train heads toward the country. He buys food at one farmhouse and takes a bath in a pond. When another farmer refuses to sell him food, Jurgis responds by destroying 100 recently planted peach trees. Jurgis becomes a professional tramp, living from day to day, working and stealing enough to get by. For the most part he is able to forget his family and his past, but when he watches a mother bathe her young son, Jurgis has an emotional breakdown.

Commentary

Literary
Device

The change in environment results in a physical change in Jurgis. For the first time in years he is able to bathe and lose the stench of the fertilizer plant from himself and his clothes. This is a symbolic baptism, a cleansing into new life. However, Sinclair does not create the typical literary pastoral, where rural life is presented in an idealized manner. Instead, some of the same problems evident in the city exist in the country, with some farmers treating animals better than they treat workers.

Jurgis' life as a tramp does refresh and revive him. This remarkable and uplifting change is the direct result of escaping the city; however, the escape cannot be permanent. One sign of the corruption and evils of capitalism follows the migratory workers: bands of prostitutes.

Glossary

wanderlust   an impulse, longing, or urge to wander or travel.

reminiscences   an account, written or spoken, of remembered experiences.

dray   a low, sturdily built cart with detachable sides, for carrying heavy loads.

debauchery   extreme indulgence of one's appetites, especially for sensual pleasure.

Chapter 23

Summary

After spending the summer as a hobo, Jurgis returns to Chicago in the fall. He finds work digging tunnels for telephone lines; in actuality, he is digging tunnels for freight trains. Jurgis breaks his arm after only a few weeks on the job and must spend two weeks in the hospital. After he is released from the hospital, Jurgis once again is out on the street in the middle of winter with no means of survival. When his money runs out, he is forced to become a beggar, but he does not do well.

Commentary

Jurgis returns to Chicago a smarter man. Without hesitation, he lies to the foreman, claiming to be from Kansas City. Soon he spends his time working underground during the day and visiting saloons at night. True to form, his good luck doesn't last. And once again fate causes misfortune in his life; this time Jurgis breaks his arm.

Again it is Christmastime, and spending the holiday alone in a hospital bed is ironically Jurgis' best Christmas in America. Only after he is released from the hospital does the reality of his situation hit him, and soon he is destitute once more. As Jurgis roams the streets as a beggar, he becomes class conscious for the first time in his life. He also begins to become suspicious of religion. Jurgis astutely wonders what the evangelists really know about sin and suffering, realizing that the poor come to meetings only to have shelter from the cold.

Glossary

camaraderie loyalty and a warm, friendly feeling among comrades.

vice evil or wicked conduct or behavior; depravity or corruption.

mendicant person who begs for money, food, clothes, etc., given to the poor.

harlot prostitute.

Chapter 24

Summary

One evening, when begging in the theater district, Jurgis encounters a drunken man who invites him back to his house. Along the way, the drunk gives Jurgis a $100 bill to pay the cab fare; Jurgis pockets the bill. The man is Freddie Jones, the son of the packer for whom Jurgis has worked. Freddie provides Jurgis with a feast of food and drink. After Freddie falls asleep, the butler kicks Jurgis out, but Jurgis still has the $100 bill.

Commentary

Instead of his usual summary narrative, Sinclair dramatizes most of this chapter. For the first time, it appears that chance benefits Jurgis. Not only is Jurgis seemingly fated to meet Freddie Jones, but Freddie forgets that he gives Jurgis a $100 bill. Just as the dramatized scene is now out of place in the novel, the entire meeting seems out of place; however, if chance is responsible for all the misfortune in Jurgis' life, then it can likewise be responsible for this one seeming piece of luck.

This encounter enables Sinclair to dramatize how the upper class lives, comparing it to the miserable existence Jurgis has had in America. Not only does this chance meeting serve as contrast of the opulent versus the indigent, it serves as an opportunity to see how Jurgis responds to his newfound wealth. Without a doubt, Jurgis pockets the bill, but what he does next is extremely telling.

Glossary

subjugate   to bring under control or subjection; conquer.

benignant   kindly or gracious, sometimes in a patronizing way.

automaton   a person or animal acting in an automatic or mechanical way.

tesselated   paved in a mosaic pattern of small, square blocks.

portiere   a curtain, usually heavy, hung in a doorway.

livery   an identifying uniform such as was formerly worn by feudal retainers or is now worn by servants or those in some particular group or trade.

insouciance   state of calm; the quality or state of being untroubled and carefree.

Chapter 25

Summary

Unable to gain lodging for the night with a $100 bill, Jurgis attempts to change it by buying a beer. The bartender, however, only provides change for a $1 bill, and a fight ensues. Jurgis winds up in jail again. In prison, Jurgis once more meets up with Jack Duane. No longer needing to provide for a wife and child, Jurgis is now able to accept Duane's worldview and vows to look him up after he serves his time.

After Jurgis is released from prison, he goes to Duane, who introduces Jurgis to the criminal world of Chicago and the inner workings of the illicit alliances among politicians, businessmen, and criminals. Buck Holloran, an acquaintance of Duane's, explains many of the inner workings of the corruption as he hires Jurgis to collect the wages of sundry city employees. After a series of illegal adventures with Duane, Jurgis meets up with Bush Harper, the man who helped Jurgis become a citizen, and eventually gets involved with politics.

Mike Scully needs to rig an election and get the workers to vote for a Republican candidate. In order to do this, he needs a man who is familiar with the stockyards and is willing and able to organize the campaign. Jurgis is that man and is soon working at Durham's. Working as a hog trimmer, Jurgis joins the union and begins to spread news about Doyle, the Republican candidate for office. Chiefly through his efforts, Doyle is elected, and the laborers mistakenly believe they have used the system to defeat a capitalist.

Commentary

Jurgis' rebellious nature, which previously has only been alluded to, is now displayed in full force. He becomes a criminal, taking full advantage of the system. And for the first time in his life, Jurgis is getting ahead in the world. Although he demonstrates a bit of sympathy for his first victim, Jurgis soon submits to the natural law of the jungle, becoming the hunter instead of the hunted.

Once again, mention is made of the Socialist Party, and once again Jurgis does not understand or care to understand the socialist position. Jurgis believes that he now has control over his destiny and is making choices that will affect his future positively. In reality, he is still being used by the higher-ups on the pecking order. This time, Scully is the one pulling all Jonas' strings.

The majority of this chapter continues the muckraking that Sinclair has been doing throughout *The Jungle*. This time, the police and government officials are the primary people being indicted. Thematically, this illustrates Sinclair's beliefs that society is severely corrupt: The business world, political world, and criminal world are all equally exploitative in nature. By the end of the chapter, Duane, who has served his purpose, disappears, driven out of town by the police.

Glossary

pugilist   boxer.

oligarchy   form of government in which the ruling power belongs to a few persons.

tenement   a building divided into apartments, now specifically in the slums that is run-down and overcrowded.

usurer   a person who lends money at interest, here specifically at a rate of interest that is excessive or unlawfully high.

firebrand   a person who stirs up others to revolt or strife.

hogshead   a large barrel or cask holding from 63 to 140 gallons.

Plutocrat   a person whose wealth is the source of control or great influence.

Chapter 26

Summary

Following Scully's advice, Jurgis keeps his job at Durham's. Scully wants him there because a strike is imminent. When the strike takes place, he then encourages Jurgis to be a scab and use the strike to his advantage. Jurgis is one of the few skilled men inside the plant during the strike. After a night of drinking and gambling, Jurgis encounters Connor. Again Jurgis assaults him; again Jurgis himself is beaten and taken to the police station. Although Bush Harper attempts to help Jurgis, Jurgis now finds out that Connor is one of Scully's right hand men. Harper convinces Jurgis to pay him as much money as he has so Harper can use it to pay off a man to reduce Jurgis's bail (Harper, of course, pockets the money) and encourages Jurgis to skip town once he is out on bail.

Commentary

A strike by meat cutters and butchers actually took place in 1904. Sinclair uses this incident as the basis for his story. Combining the facts of the strike with the facts of corruption, Sinclair accurately presents life at the turn of the century in Chicago. In fact, critics and historians rarely dispute his presentation of this information. Only the accuracy of Sinclair's descriptions of the extreme working conditions and abuses presented within the meatpacking plants are consistently questioned and debated. The strike in 1904 failed for the same reasons presented in *The Jungle*: dishonest negotiations between management and labor, the flood of workers into the market, and the increase of product prices while the prices of raw materials are forced down. The fact that the majority of the jobs required only unskilled labor also affected the workers' chance at a decent strike settlement.

Style & Language

During the strike, Sinclair continues his use of summary narrative, and in doing so, he presents the black scabs as if they, too, are animals, showing no insight or appreciation for black culture. Thematically, this is important because it shows the greed of the packers, who hire anyone as long as the packers themselves keep making a profit. It also shows, ironically, the similarity between the workers and the packers: Everyone is class conscious and recognizes a superior or inferior group of people based on assumptions and misinformation. Whether this view is Sinclair's own is not as clear. The omniscient narrator speaks of the blacks as a collective group, and Sinclair offers no insight into individual thoughts and feelings. Historically, at the turn of the century, the Socialist Party was not particularly interested in the well-being and advancement of African Americans.

As for Jurgis, again fate intervenes, and all of his good fortune is lost due to one chance meeting with Connor. Initially, this appears to be yet another loss for the hardworking protagonist; however, this chance meeting actually enables Jurgis to discover socialism. In doing so, Jurgis realizes that socialism alone provides a way out of the capitalistic problems he has encountered throughout his life in America.

Glossary

arbitration   the settlement of a dispute by a person or persons chosen to hear both sides and come to a decision.

labyrinthine   having an intricate network of winding passages hard to follow without losing one's way.

pell-mell   in a jumbled, confused mass or manner; without order or method.

helter-skelter   in a disorderly, hurried manner.

kimono   a loose dressing gown.

smote   to have struck or hit hard.

Joliet   referring to a prison located in the town of the same name in northeast Illinois.

Chapter 27

Summary

More than any of his previous times on the streets, Jurgis is in no physical condition to improve his situation. Jurgis is mindful of all he had and all he has lost. In order to stay warm, he attends a political meeting. He falls asleep, and is tossed into the street because of his snoring. He starts begging and by chance meets a woman who attended his wedding. She gives him Marija's address.

Just as Jurgis arrives at a large house inquiring about Marija, the police arrive and storm the dwelling. Jurgis realizes the house is a brothel and Marija is now working as a prostitute. From Marija he learns of Stanislovas' death and that Marija is addicted to morphine. Marija also tells Jurgis that the family does not blame him for running away, though she personally thinks many of their problems could have been avoided if Jurgis had allowed Ona to continue with Connor. Jurgis is jailed with the other men but is released the next morning.

Commentary

As with all naturalistic fiction (writing that depicts life as it truly is, not glossing over unsavory details), Sinclair documents the unsavory side of life in Chicago, presenting both life on the streets and life in a brothel. This chapter is the low point for Jurgis and his family. Jurgis' chance encounter with the "belle" from his wedding feast, who is not married but in a "good place," enables him to locate Marija.

Marija's descent into hell is the embodiment of Sinclair's major theme: that capitalism is a horrible system comprised of those who are users and those who are used. Women are victims who are forced into selling their bodies as a means of survival.

Marija voices this theme when she tells Jurgis, "When people are starving . . . and they have anything with a price, they ought to sell it." She accepts this as a matter of course, as the way of the world. Her words express Sinclair's view of capitalism.

But Jurgis does not readily accept this. He does not like the fact that Marija feels prostitution is her only option; though, for the first time, he realizes that is exactly what he had been doing to himself. During his night in jail, Jurgis contemplates the difficult existence his family has had in Chicago, remembering lost emotions, longing for a way out of his current predicament.

Glossary

besiege   to close in on; crowd around.

silk-stocking   a member of the wealthy or aristocratic class.

verities   principles, beliefs, etc., taken to be fundamentally and permanently true.

deshabille   the state of being only partially dressed.

chafing   being or becoming vexed, irritated, or impatient.

Chapter 28

Summary

Reluctant to face Elzbieta while still unemployed, Jurgis impulsively attends another political meeting. This time, when he falls asleep, instead of being kicked out, he is encouraged to listen. Jurgis does listen and feels as if the powerful, persuasive voice is directing his comments directly to him. The speaker awakens old dreams and desires, long dormant within Jurgis' soul, and persuades Jurgis not to accept defeat.

Commentary

This chapter serves as the climax of the novel, marking Jurgis' transition from the Old World to the New World; however, the New World is not America but rather, socialism. Serving as a contrast to the brothel, the symbol of capitalism in the previous chapter, Jurgis has an epiphany at a political meeting, the symbolic setting for socialism and change. For the first time in his life, Jurgis is willing to listen to the rhetoric of socialism, and the message moves him.

The idea of socialism appeals to Jurgis, and he must find out more. This radical change in both character and tone is one of the major weaknesses of *The Jungle*. Because Sinclair has been using summary narrative, readers know nothing about the personal side of Jurgis. His radical departure from his normal behavior goes against everything that Sinclair has presented about Jurgis before, and therefore, rings false. Sinclair has made references, albeit small ones, to socialism throughout the text, but now he goes beyond introducing the ideology to making it the major emphasis of the final three chapters. Moreover, therein lies another problem with *The Jungle*. Sinclair's flawed story ends up dismissing Jurgis, his family, and the plight of immigrants for the sake of socialism. Sinclair abandons his characters and his narrative for the sake of a political treatise.

Style & Language

The end of this chapter also marks the end of pure Zolaism. The discovery of hope and the revival of Jurgis' manhood is exactly opposite to the typically Zolaist hero who goes down in defeat. In doing this, Sinclair states that socialism is the answer to realism as well as capitalism. Marija and Jurgis illustrate the dichotomy between the two: Marija is still trapped and is therefore the victim while Jurgis escapes, becoming an activist.

Glossary

absinthe   green, bitter, toxic liqueur made with wormwood oil and anise: now illegal in most countries.

garret   the space, room, or rooms just below the roof of a house; attic.

blandishments   flattering or ingratiating acts or remarks, meant to persuade.

Chapter 29

Summary

After the speech is over, Jurgis makes his way backstage to meet the speaker. The speaker, recognizing Jurgis' desire to learn more, introduces Jurgis to Comrade Ostrinski. Ostrinski shares his own experiences and history as he takes Jurgis back to his own house. Ostrinski explains socialism to Jurgis from the point of view of a workingman. From both Ostrinski and party literature, Jurgis is able to make meaning out of his Packingtown experiences and sees socialism as the light—as the only means of salvation for all people.

Commentary

Jurgis' conversion is the key, as he acquires a new dignity, something he lost during his time in Packingtown. An unintended effect, though, is that readers are not inclined to believe or accept this transformation. Every time things start to look as though they may work out for Jurgis, something else happens, which only makes his situation worse. Readers can accept that socialism provides both hope and promise for Jurgis' future, but are not convinced that socialism is a positive and meaningful reality. Sinclair has spent too much time showing the harsh reality of Jurgis' world to expect readers to accept a chance for salvation. Jurgis' change is effective in propaganda but not effective in a novel.

Ostrinski symbolizes the heroic, working proletariat; he is the embodiment of all workers. He exists solely to be the voice of socialism from the workingman's perspective. As he explains socialism to Jurgis, he simultaneously explains it to the readers.

Glossary

Marseillaise   the national anthem of France, composed in 1792 during the French Revolution.

Tolstoy   Leo Tolstoy (1828–1910) Russian novelist whose most famous works, *War and Peace* and *Anna Karenina*, are examples of realistic fiction.

proletarian   a member of the proletariat, the working class, especially the industrial working class.

incarnation   any person or thing serving as the type or embodiment of a quality or concept.

Chapter 30

Summary

With his newfound faith and fire, Jurgis goes to see Elzbieta. She is not interested in his politics but notices the spark of industry in his eyes and tolerates his rhetoric. Soon Jurgis finds a job as a porter at a hotel, a hotel that, coincidentally, is a political hotbed of socialism. The proprietor of the hotel, Tommy Hinds, and his staff educate Jurgis and others in the ways and means of socialism. Gradually, socialism becomes the root of Jurgis' existence.

Commentary

Jurgis is like any new convert: He is fanatical about his new belief. socialism becomes the answer to all of life's problems. From a literary perspective, this chapter is too contrived: Jurgis just happens to find employment at a hotel whose proprietor is one of the leaders of the socialist movement. Throughout *The Jungle* chance has played a major part in the events of Jurgis' life, but only after Jurgis embraces socialism does a chance encounter end up benefiting him.

Sinclair also refers to the newspaper *Appeal to Reason*, rightfully acknowledging it as a propaganda paper. Later, Sinclair claims that the *Appeal* could be serious, but he does not afford a way for readers to distinguish between the two. This mirrors a problem with *The Jungle* itself. The fictional accounts gloss over the seriousness of the novel, resulting in a piece of propaganda rather than an enduring literary accomplishment.

Glossary

Trojan   here alluding to the Greek legend of the Trojan horse, a huge, hollow wooden horse Greek soldiers hid in then left at the gates of Troy; the Trojans brought the horse into the city, and the soldiers crept out and opened the gates to the rest of the Greek army, which destroyed the city of Troy.

dyspepsia   indigestion.

Octopus   reference to the novel *The Octopus*, written by Frank Norris, in which farmers fought against the railroad monopoly.

recalcitrant   hard to handle or deal with.

unregenerate   not converted to a particular belief or viewpoint.

paternalism   the principle or system of governing or controlling a country or group of employees in a manner suggesting a father's relationship with his children.

Chapter 31

Summary

Soon after getting his job, Jurgis returns to Marija, imploring her to leave the brothel, but she refuses. She is addicted to morphine and cannot find work anywhere else. Jurgis reluctantly departs, returning home to a sick Elzbieta and her unruly sons, but this time, instead of leaving, Jurgis turns to socialism for support.

Members of the Socialist Party in Chicago are preparing for the election. On the night before the vote, a millionaire sympathetic to the socialist movement invites Jurgis to dinner. Here Jurgis encounters Lucas, an evangelist, and Nicholas Schliemann, a former philosophy professor, who debate the nature of socialism while answering questions for a skeptical magazine editor.

Jurgis attends a party gathering the next day to watch election returns. The Socialist Party makes substantial gains across the country, especially in Packingtown. One socialist leader interprets the results as a call for further organization by party members, for the voters may not really be socialists, but rather just disgruntled democrats. *The Jungle* closes with the orator inciting the crowd with chants of "*Chicago will be ours!* CHICAGO WILL BE OURS!"

Commentary

Marija cannot leave her new life. This harsh reality is evident, and for her to do so would undermine everything else in the text. Although socialism is the only hope for the working person, Marija does not see this. She has reluctantly accepted the way of a capitalistic society and has become both unwilling and unable to change.

New characters discuss the two major aspects of socialism—its religious and scientific implications. Some embrace socialism as a new religion, replacing Christianity, while others favor the efficiency, rationality, and order of the new system, believing it superior to all other forms of government. The dialogue between Schliemann and Lucas does nothing to further the plot and does not include Jurgis at all; rather, they voice Sinclair's opinions, becoming a sounding board for the pro-socialist movement.

The statistics at the end of the novel mirror actual results of the presidential election of 1904. Although the socialists view the number of votes they received as a significant increase from the past election, the actual number of votes was statistically quite low. In the original serial form of *The Jungle*, Jurgis is arrested on election night; however, this ending does not emphasize a socialist triumph, and Sinclair changed the ending when *The Jungle* was published in book form.

Glossary

itinerant   traveling from place to place or on a circuit.

stygian   dark or gloomy.

chloroform   to kill with chloroform, a toxic, cancer-causing, colorless, volatile liquid that has a sweet taste.

zealot   a person who is ardently devoted to a purpose; fanatic.

anarchist   a person who promotes anarchy, or political disorder, as by flouting or ignoring rules, duties, or accepted standards of conduct.

catchpenny   made merely to sell; cheap and flashy.

pettifogger   a lawyer who handles petty cases, especially one who uses unethical methods in conducting trumped-up cases.

chicanery   the use of clever but tricky talk or action to deceive or evade, as in legal dealings.

CHARACTER ANALYSES

The Narrator 76

Jurgis 77

Ona 79

Marija 80

Elzbieta 81

Phil Connor 81

Jack Duane 82

When completing a character analysis, first determine the type of character being analyzed and then recognize how the author applied the various methods of characterization. To establish character type, identify whether the character is major or minor, flat or round, and static or dynamic. *Major characters* are the primary characters in the novel, and the *minor characters* play a supporting role. *Flat characters* tend to be stereotypes whereas *round characters* show enough different characteristics to seem believable. *Static characters* remain the same; *dynamic characters* experience either a personality or attitudinal change during the course of the novel. Classifying characters this way is the initial step in determining the role of the individual character in the greater scheme of the text. After determining the type of character, assess how the author develops that character. The easiest way to analyze a character is to examine what a character says and does. Usually these words and actions are governed by the thoughts of the character. In addition, a physical description of a character is often quite telling, as is what other characters say about the character. Finally, what a narrator states about a character is also extremely revealing.

Classical critical interpretations of *The Jungle* usually emphasize Sinclair's novel as a work of propaganda, and, therefore, consider the characters solely *illustrative* in nature; that is, Sinclair uses them as a means to an end in order to illustrate his point. These interpretations consider the characters in a narrow range rather than a broad spectrum and do not consider them overly essential to a discussion of the text. Traditionally, rounded, dynamic characters are favored over flat and static ones because critics value realistic fiction, and in reality, people are complex and multi-dimensional; however, another view exists. Some critics compare *The Jungle* to Victorian novels, which also had omniscient narrators. In the Victorian era, the novel was a new literary form and characters were not always fully developed or well-rounded. In fact, in order to complete fairly an assessment of the characters in *The Jungle*, the narrator must be examined first.

The Narrator

Although not truly a character, the narrator of *The Jungle* supplies the most important voice. Because *The Jungle* is told from a third-person, omniscient point of view, insight into what a character thinks, says, and does isn't available firsthand. Readers are told what happens; therefore, the most telling information readers gain into Jurgis and his family is from the narrator.

Readers need to remember, though, that being all-knowing is not the same as providing reliable or truthful information. The narrator of *The Jungle*, clearly taking on Sinclair's voice, has a socialist agenda and therefore only reveals what is sympathetic to the socialist cause. The intrusions the narrator makes in the text are glimpses into the thoughts of the characters and they unquestionably shape the characters; readers need to remember to remain objective, especially when the narrator does not. The narrator of *The Jungle* has a socialist bias, although this bias is not revealed until the end of the text; therefore, readers must understand that the commentary provided during early chapters is designed to make the reader unknowingly sympathetic to the socialist movement.

Jurgis

The main character of *The Jungle*, Jurgis, is the only character to appear in every chapter. Although most of the action in the text is shown from his perspective, readers actually gain very little insight into Jurgis' innermost person. This does not mean, however, that as a character he is not a sufficient study. Indeed, because readers have no firsthand knowledge of Jurgis' thoughts, beliefs, feelings, and passions, he is quite different from most characters in modern novels—he is neither developed nor complex—but he is still worthy of analysis.

Sinclair primarily depicts Jurgis as a protagonist as defined by Emile Zola; that is, one who is the victim of chance and whose fate is determined by forces beyond his control. Because Emile Zola both created and mastered this type of fiction, the style is known as *Zolaism* (and is also called *naturalism*). At the end of the novel, however, Jurgis does experience a change, and becomes a dynamic character; one who is proactive and embraces socialism as a means of escaping the drudgery of his existence.

From the onset, and throughout the entire text, Jurgis is shy and awkward at social functions. This is a mark of his staunch individualism, a trait simultaneously beneficial and harmful to him. Early on he is a strapping young man, full of vigor and life, and is able to carry himself through any adversity. This physical description provides more insight into his character because Jurgis experiences both a physical and emotional change. Gradually, the difficulties he encounters wear him down. In one sense, *The Jungle* is similar to a medieval morality play, and Jurgis is a contemporary "Everyman." The characters in morality plays were symbolic representations, used to illustrate an idea; Jurgis represents all immigrants. His experiences are typical of immigrants, and his struggles are their struggles. By presenting Jurgis in a sympathetic light, Sinclair enables readers to embrace all immigrants. *The Jungle* reveals the problems that all immigrants and poor people suffer, and presents socialism as the solution.

In addition to being an Everyman, Jurgis is a *literary naïf*, or naïve person. He starts out as innocent and trusting, but gradually grows wise to the ways of the world. Jurgis' transformation is gradual, mirroring his gradual acceptance of socialism. Before Jurgis is able to exploit the system, the system must exploit him. Before he can accept socialism, he must experience and be victimized by another economic system, in this case, capitalism. Through experience, Jurgis learns that everything is not as it seems, and that blind faith is not necessarily a good thing.

As Jurgis grows distrustful of the economic system in which he is enslaved, he realizes that he enjoys his family, particularly his son, only when he's not working. Unfortunately, for Jurgis and his family, when he is unemployed, his family suffers financially. This relates to a larger theme—the effect the capitalistic system has on both workers and the family unit. Jurgis' relationship with his family demonstrates that the capitalistic system, of which he is enslaved, is contrary to and in fact destroys the family unit.

Jurgis' personal loss of family leads to his own rebellion. His first action—destroying peach trees—is reactive, striking out against the farmer's insults. Eventually, Jurgis becomes proactive, but his life of crime is not very productive. After he returns to the city, Jurgis becomes as much a man for hire as Ona had been, illustrating the double standard of the day. Jurgis' life of crime is his attempt at getting back at the city that got him. Nevertheless, his old feelings remain, and when he sees Connor again, Jurgis' true feelings about the sanctity of marriage and love of family re-surface.

Later, discovering the truth about Marija enables Jurgis to establish more firmly his true feelings about what is right and wrong in the world. Because he was unable to save Ona, he longs to save Marija. Attending a socialist meeting by chance leads Jurgis to rebel constructively. By the end of *The Jungle*, Jurgis is satisfied with his place in society and is confident that he can help improve society for everyone. He realizes that alone, as an individual, he cannot expect to accomplish much;

however, as an individual who comprises part of a larger group, he can accomplish many things. In the beginning of the novel, Jurgis is driven by his desire to work harder; at the end of the novel, he is driven by the desire to work harder for the socialist movement.

Ona

Although at the onset Ona appears to be the complete opposite of Jurgis, she actually is quite like him: Both are traditional naturalistic characters; that is, the typical characters in naturalistic fiction—those who will be exploited. As a naturalistic woman, Ona eventually succumbs to the problems of a capitalistic society, turning to prostitution and eventually dying. Even though she is a stock (flat, stereotypical) character, Ona is the character on whom readers often take the most pity.

Physically, Ona is frail and frightened. She is overwhelmed most of the time. Initially, she is unable to leave Lithuania without her family, so Elzbieta and her children join Ona and Jurgis, as does Marija. This desire to stay with family is a positive trait. In Chicago, she works to keep her Old World order in her New World. Throughout her life in Packingtown, Ona works to keep her family together. She wants both Jurgis and her family to succeed in America, and when his earnings alone are not enough, she gets a job. Like Jurgis, she works hard but is unable to protect and provide for her family.

Ona's representation of the weaker sex is not surprising; in fact, Sinclair uses typical stereotypes. A big surprise, however, is the fact that Ona is able to keep secrets from her husband. In doing so, she exhibits strength of character in contrast to her general weakness. First, her secret actions are a sacrifice for the good of the family. She correctly realizes that Connor has the ability to ruin the family, and therefore agrees to his demands. Second, knowing how Jurgis will react, she keeps the secret of her forced adultery from him. She even returns to work a mere week after giving birth, permanently ruining her health—another sacrifice made by the seemingly frail woman, who supposedly needs guidance and protection from others.

Some readers have difficulty accepting Ona's actions and overall show of strength. For most of the novel she is depicted as being frail and alone. She is the one who Jurgis must protect and care for—a member of the fairer sex who needs a man to provide for her. She's presented in contrast to Marija, who is a strong woman. Ona's actions fit, however, in the greater analogy running throughout the text: In the jungle, a mother fights to the death to protect her young. Ona does what she must—even having an affair with Connor—in an attempt to keep her family employed and therefore fed and sheltered. Even during a time when Ona is being presented as weak and frail, she is actually exhibiting a great strength. It is ironic that the protected, in a way, becomes the protector.

Of course, Ona dies, but before this happens, it is necessary for the system to pressure her into "sexual slavery by her economic masters." Because of the economic slavery, Ona is unable to be an effective wife and mother. This worldview, although consistent with all naturalistic literature, appears in *The Jungle* to serve Sinclair's purpose of promoting socialism. Ona serves as a negative example for the value of capitalism.

Marija

At the beginning of *The Jungle*, Marija serves almost as a female Jurgis. She is concerned not only with the traditional Lithuanian customs but also the manner in which the customs are carried out. Like Jurgis, in the beginning she has faith in hard work and believes individuals can achieve success and prosperity through their own efforts. Like Jurgis, she is enthusiastic about the union, until she learns that the union is powerless against the Beef Trust. She, like Jurgis, suffers a physical injury on the job, and this limits her subsequent employment opportunities. Unlike Jurgis, she eventually succumbs to the pressures of her economic situation, defeated.

The degree to which Marija is similar to Jurgis is the degree to which she initially appears to be different from other women. Early on she is strong and makes a good wage, but that changes. The first sign of change is her inability to have her own wedding, especially after seeing to the details of Jurgis and Ona's: Fate forces her to remain alone. Her entire relationship with Tamoszius illustrates the effects of an industrialized society on love relationships. Because of financial problems, love is unable to prosper.

Losing her love relationship, combined with her physical injury, eventually leads to Marija's spiritual death. Early on, she is a pillar of strength, forcing people to dance when they are tired, speaking out against horrible conditions, and enduring job after job in order to make money. Early on, she believes in hard work and its results. By the end of *The Jungle*, she has no strength left and accepts her fate as a prostitute as inevitable.

Her acceptance of prostitution, even stating that Ona could have saved the family, reveals the depths to which she sinks. Her willingness to remain a whore addicted to morphine shows that, more than any other character in *The Jungle*, Marija suffers as a result of the capitalistic system at work.

Early on, Marija is a foil for Ona. Marija is an extremely active woman, whereas Ona is quite passive. At the same time, Marija is an ironic foil for Jurgis. In an age of male dominance, she is exceeding him in her success. In the end of the novel, however, Jurgis has the positive metamorphosis. It is as if she embraces the role of the victim and allows the forces of nature to defeat her entirely—body and soul. Her fate is the embodiment of the naturalistic woman.

Elzbieta

Although a minor character, Elzbieta is an important one, for she is the embodiment of the Old World. In Elzbieta, Sinclair creates a character who suffers in silence. She endures the loss of her family, especially her children, with a stoic acceptance. Like Ona, she desires to do what it takes to keep her family together. When necessary, she lies for her son, so Stanislovas is able to work when he is legally too young. She is a stay-at-home mom for as long as she can be, but when the situation calls for her to get a job, she does so. When she doesn't have enough money to bury her children, she is not above begging from neighbors to get what she needs. Elzbieta's strength of character is in her ability to endure; but enduring is not the same as living As a minor character, Elzbieta is the embodiment of this minor theme of *The Jungle*.

Phil Connor

Phil Connor is the embodiment of all corrupt evil in the industrialized world. He is both the typical and stereotypical boss who uses his power and influence to get what he wants. When Ona refuses to sleep with him of her own free will, he threatens the economic stability of her entire family, so that she has no choice but to give in. Connor's exploitation of Ona serves as a microcosm of how the entire industry works: The bosses exploit the laborers.

After Jurgis justifiably attacks Connor, Connor gets a continuance, subsequently lies in court, and finally blacklists Jurgis. This illustrates the power money has in the judicial system. Not only does Connor perjure himself in court, he is able to supply witnesses; the court sides with Connor before the trial even begins. After Jurgis serves his time, his inability to get a job serves not only as an additional punishment for him, it is a lesson for others who may attempt to strike out against oppression. Ironically, Connor, who is seemingly the reason for Jurgis' downfall, also seemingly serves as his salvation. Without encountering Connor again, the chain of events that leads Jurgis to socialism, would not have occurred.

Jack Duane

Jack Duane is the closest thing Jurgis has to a friend in the entire novel. It is quite appropriate that Jurgis meets Duane in jail, for this is an ironic statement: Jurgis has to go to jail in order to become a criminal. Outside of prison, Jurgis is an honest man. Only after he is sentenced for his "crimes" does Jurgis go to a place where he learns how to break the law.

A minor character, Duane is nonetheless significant. In order for the thematic nature of *The Jungle* to be evident, Jurgis has to explore all options available to him. Joining the underworld of Chicago crime enables Jurgis to experience economic success, and eventually realize the price of success. When Duane is no longer necessary, he is conveniently sacrificed—both by the mob and by Upton Sinclair.

CRITICAL
ESSAYS

The Tenets of Sinclair's Socialism 84

Jurgis' Journey through Hell
to Socialism 85

Sinclair's *The Jungle* from a
Contemporary Critical Perspective   . . .87

The Tenets of Sinclair's Socialism

Socialism is both an economic and social doctrine, and the political movement inspired by this doctrine. The basic premise argues for the nationalization of natural resources and utilities while calling for state ownership and distribution of wealth. Most important, socialism wants to create a global, classless cooperative of all people.

Originally, the terms *socialism* and *communism* were used interchangeably. However, communism is an extreme form of socialism that advocates the entire elimination of capitalism. Many communists continue to use the term socialist even though socialists distance themselves from what they call "authoritarian tyranny." Most socialists recognize a need for private ownership and only advocate the need for state ownership and operation of the vital components of society.

The worsening conditions of the proletariat, or working class, during the close of the nineteenth century led to the modern socialist movement. When the predicted violent revolution did not occur, many socialists began to reject the need for violence as a means for achieving their goals. This ideological shift separated the socialists from the Marxists (communists). The German writer Eduard Bernstein wrote about the basic beliefs of attaining socialist goals through reformist, parliamentary, and evolutionary methods rather than through revolution.

Sinclair's goal was to attain what he referred to as "democratic socialism" in the United States. Although most readers did not realize it, his beliefs actually embraced the American dream. In fact, what Sinclair wanted was a return to the original idea that inspired immigrants and freedom-seekers—a return to the original American dream. In one of his most famous passages, he writes, "Passionately, more than words can utter, I love this land of mine. . . . There never was any land like it—there may never be any like it again; and Freedom watches from her mountains, trembling." Sinclair loved what the United States stood for but was concerned that the economic system of capitalism was interfering with the premises and promises of liberty that the founding fathers sought. Sinclair based his attack on capitalism on his belief that capitalism violated essential American values.

Sinclair believed that socialism was the means for American liberals to achieve most fully the ideals they embraced. Sinclair abhorred the exploitation of the working class and economic inequality. He thought that America should be the land of opportunity for all people, provided they were willing to work. A strong work ethic was imperative. "If a fellow won't work, he has no right to anything." However, when a worker, like Jurgis, is willing to work and is able to work but cannot work, that is a problem. Or when an entire family is working but not succeeding, that too is a problem.

Sinclair's form of socialism dominated his writings as he attempted to provide a logical argument for what was, to him, a very personal and emotional issue. For Sinclair, the ideals of America stressed equality and brotherhood, but in all actuality, the rich did indeed get richer and the poor got poorer. No equality. No brotherhood. But just as *The Jungle* was seen as an attack on the meatpacking industry, Sinclair's perceived views on capitalism and socialism endured more so than his actual message. Too many people are unable to separate a political system from an economic system. Moreover, the United States, unlike many European counterparts, never had an overwhelmingly successful socialist movement, so Sinclair is remembered as a muckraker, not a socialist.

Jurgis' Journey through Hell to Socialism

Toward the end of *The Jungle*, when Jurgis stumbles into the socialist meeting that later changes his life, many critics complain that his transformation is too swift, too sudden, too unbelievable. Yet, that evangelical, emotional, immediate conversion is exactly what Upton Sinclair intended. Jurgis is able to accept immediately what he hears and to convert fully to this new line of thinking because he has already followed a pattern of believing in things and having these things betray him. By the time Jurgis converts to socialism at the end of *The Jungle*, he has no other options. He has been longing for someone or something to provide him with answers to what is wrong with the world. He is unable to follow Marija's acceptance of the way of the world, but has nothing to counter her arguments until he finds the rhetoric of socialism. Although Jurgis does not pray, socialism is the answer to his prayers.

It is no coincidence that Sinclair mentions Dante in Chapter 9. In *The Divine Comedy*, Dante's masterpiece, readers join the poet's quest for salvation. Dante's *Comedy*, like *The Jungle*, begins in despair and ends in bliss, takes a realistic view of human nature, and is written in practical and not poetic language (Italian not Latin). *The Comedy* is a journey through the land of the dead, and similarly, Jurgis journeys through the hell of the industrialized urban jungle. Both *The Comedy* and *The Jungle* are meant to be read on both literal and allegorical levels, as poet and packer both search for salvation. At the end of their journeys, Dante and Jurgis find paradise, Dante's in heaven and Jurgis' in socialism.

In addition to Jurgis' life in America being a symbolic journey, the religious implications throughout *The Jungle* are apparent. Dante travels through hell in order to reach redemption. Throughout *The Jungle*, Jurgis is searching for something to believe in, to provide a purpose for his life. That is what religion provides people. In the beginning, Jurgis puts faith in himself and his own work ethic. From the days in the Lithuanian forest to his wedding night, Jurgis vows "to work harder." This belief in his ability to be solely successful and responsible carries him for quite a while. In addition to his belief in himself, Jurgis believes in the American dream. His faith in himself and his new country lasts only so long; eventually, reality catches up with him, and he realizes he cannot do everything himself.

At times, Jurgis puts his faith in his family, allowing his relationships to sustain him. When he is unable to work, the only solace he finds is with his wife and child, but Ona betrays him and their love (so he thinks) and soon after, their son dies. After losing the two most important people in his life, he decides again to rely only on himself. This time, though, his faith in himself is not as a worker but as an abuser of the system that has, for so long, abused him. He turns to alcohol but finds no comfort. Then he turns to a life of crime. For a short time, Jurgis believes that cheating the system is the answer. This neither works nor leaves him fulfilled.

Throughout his journey through the jungle, the judicial system, the economic system, and his personal moral system all fail Jurgis. Ironically, no real mention of a religious strength exists. Early on, a priest vouches for the legal age of Stanislovas, but that is the extent of Jurgis' religious life. The primary reason for this exclusion is that American democratic socialism embraces the teachings of Jesus. In essence, Sinclair presents socialism as a new religion. Sinclair completes this extended metaphor by comparing Jurgis to the disciple Paul. Both men have a religious epiphany. Jurgis' sudden conversion and immediate espousal of socialism serves as his baptism, and like all new converts, he seeks to share his good news with others.

Throughout *The Jungle*, Jurgis searches for answers, for something that can provide guidance for his entire existence. Everything that he believed in earlier in his life fails him, so it is no wonder that when he experiences an alternative that dismisses everything he previously embraced, he is immediately attracted to it. Socialism is the answer to all the questions and problems Jurgis has, whether he knew it or not. This is made quite clear when it comes to the issue of alcohol. Capitalism leads men to drink; a drinking socialist causes his boss to fire him.

The final chapters of *The Jungle* serve as an intellectual inquiry into this newfound religion. When Jurgis is converted, Sinclair needs to provide the theology for both the new convert in the book (Jurgis) and the new converts who read the book (all readers). This is one of the reasons why the final three chapters of *The Jungle* have no real narrative and read more like a treatise.

Readers may notice that Sinclair sows the seeds of socialism throughout the text—through characters like Tamoszius and Grandmother Majauszkiene and events such as socialists running for office. However, until Jurgis is ready to embrace the message, (a sinner only needs to recognize his sin); merely hearing the message will do him no good. Everything else must prove to be fruitless before Jurgis is willing even to listen to something so contrary to his former way of thinking and his former life. Ironically, like all new religious converts, Jurgis is unable to convince everyone he has found the truth. His family members need their own epiphanies.

Sinclair's *The Jungle* from a Contemporary Critical Perspective

The traditional, scholarly approach toward literary analysis focuses solely on the structure of a literary work in order to determine both its worth and its meaning. This school of literary analysis is known as *New Criticism*. New Critics focus on the written work isolated from everything else because, they believe that, by closely examining the way the author uses language, one is eventually able to establish the true meaning of the work. A series of close readings focusing on the author's ability to use words is the means of appreciating and valuing works; therefore, New Critics focus on the aesthetics of literature when making an evaluation.

The *aesthetics* of a novel include the way an author uses elements of style, such as imagery, irony, and paradox, to enhance characters, plot, and theme. From this perspective, *The Jungle* is not considered quality literature. New Critics argue that Sinclair uses the form of the novel to promote his political agenda at the expense of his art. Lack of character development, inconsistency in tone and voice, and the loss of narrative at the end are just a few of the criticisms raised against *The Jungle*.

This lack of aesthetics mixed with an unpopular message resulted in a lack of respect for *The Jungle* in literary circles. Throughout most of the twentieth century, most critics considered Sinclair's book as either propaganda or muckraking—no more and no less. Most critics considered the majority of Sinclair's works of fiction in this manner; therefore, his reputation as a serious novelist was not high. However, as literary theory and critics advanced and changed, so too did the perception of *The Jungle*.

One of the primary critiques of New Criticism is that this literary theory isolates a work from the world in which it was created. Although focusing on the structure of a work is an important aspect of literary analysis in an educational system, this technique is inherently problematic because this isolation prevents critics from understanding the work in relation to the society that created it. More recent trends in literary theory argue that New Criticism should be the starting point rather than the end of literary analysis. Many contemporary critics attempt to re-establish literature's place in the world by focusing on the relationship between works and the culture in which they are created.

These "cultural critics" prefer to use the term *texts* instead of *works* and view their criticism as "a practice rather than a doctrine." The value of literature, for cultural critics, exceeds the actual words on the page. New Critics tend to focus on and value only poetical language whereas cultural critics focus on and value both poetical and literal language. For cultural critics, what is traditionally referred to as literature is neither superior nor inferior to the non-literary works of a particular period. Instead of literature consisting of a body of works, it consists of a set of texts that act as models for that particular culture. Texts are created within a culture and therefore must be examined within the context of that culture.

Culture is the complex means by which a society produces and simultaneously reproduces itself; texts are the means of reproduction. Therefore, texts are not only an expression of a view of a culture: They also help create that culture's view. This endless chain of events is easily illustrated by examining the historical impact of *The Jungle*.

When Upton Sinclair visited the stockyards in Chicago, that industrial culture provided the raw materials for his text for *The Jungle* (an example of culture creating text). However, when *The Jungle* was printed, its content so affected the reading population that an immediate outcry against the meatpackers ensued (text creating culture). Before the publication of *The Jungle*, the majority of the meat eating, reading public had no idea of the atrocities within the industry. Also, generations reading *The Jungle* 100 years after its initial publication have no idea of the horrors that existed, and for the most part, only have Sinclair's text to illustrate these horrors. The text continues to influence culture, regardless of its accuracy or immediacy.

In addition to illustrating the dynamic relationship between culture and text, *The Jungle* also shows the relative unimportance of authorial intention when it comes to literary analysis. Sinclair's primary focus of socialism did not take hold with readers of his own era, nor did it provide any lasting impression on future generations; yet the continued claim to fame for *The Jungle* is its exposure of abuse in the meatpacking industry. Instead of having just one integral meaning, texts can have multiple meanings.

Cultural critics see *The Jungle* as a text that is both representative of time and place as well as simultaneously having an effect on future cultures. They recognize that Sinclair's form did not adhere to traditional genres, so he effectively created his own medium. His text created a kind of power over the industry and was a means of change. Contemporary critics view literature as more than just an autonomous piece of writing isolated from the rest of the world. This does not mean that contemporary critics routinely dismiss literary style and the use of irony, paradox, and metaphor. Rather, they examine how particular texts use (or do not use) particular devices and determine how this affects the reception of a text. Some texts have universal appeal; others are limited to a particular sub-culture within a culture. But all are important. Unlike New Criticism, which tends to be an academic affair, cutting a work off from society, cultural criticism attempts to save and value literature by acknowledging its significance.

CliffsNotes Review

Use this CliffsNotes Review to test your understanding of the original text. Working through the question sections and the Practice Projects puts you well on your way to understanding a comprehensive and meaningful interpretation of Sinclair's *The Jungle*.

Q&A

1. In what American city is Packingtown located?

2. What is the largest financial mistake that Jurgis and his family make?

3. Jurgis is jailed for attacking whom?

4. With whom does Jurgis team up for a life of crime?

5. At the end of *The Jungle,* what is Marija working as?

Answers: (1) Chicago. (2) buying a house. (3) Phil Connor, Ona's boss. (4) Jack Duane. (5) a prostitute.

Identify the Quote

1. "I will work harder."

2. "I did not want—to do it," she said; "I tried—I tried not to do it. I only did it—to save us. It was our only chance."

3. "It's the second time they've sent me up on a trumped-up charge—I've had hard luck and can't pay them what they want. Why don't you quit Chicago with me, Jurgis?"

4. "When people are starving," the other continued, "and they have anything with a price, they ought to sell it, I say. I guess you realize it now when it's too late. Ona could have taken care of us all, in the beginning."

5. "You know what to do about it—vote the socialist ticket!"

Answers: (1) Jurgis, whenever he is faced with adversity early in the novel. (2) Ona to Jurgis, explaining her forced adultery. (3) Jack Duane to Jurgis, the second time they meet in prison. (4) Marija to Jurgis, explaining her acceptance of prostitution, illustrating her unwillingness to change. (5) Tommy Hinds, in his remedy for all the evils of the world, from failure in business to a quarrelsome mother-in-law.

Essay Questions

1. How is the title of *The Jungle* both symbolic and representative of life in Packingtown?

2. Is *The Jungle* an effective piece of persuasive writing, convincing readers of the validity of socialism? Why or why not?

3. How does Sinclair's use of an omniscient, intrusive narrator affect a reader's appreciation for *The Jungle*? How does this all-knowing narrator affect the development of characters, plot, and themes?

Practice Project

Create a Web page that debates the status of Upton Sinclair and *The Jungle* in the history of American literature. This project should serve both as a review and a culminating activity for your study of the text.

Use a variety of search engines, such as yahoo.com or searchalot.com, to find appropriate links. Consider page design as well as content. A well-designed page helps you organize your own thoughts as well as provide easier access for others. This project has two major steps:

1. Explore the life of Upton Sinclair, the history of unions and strikes, the popular response to *The Jungle*, and criticism about the literary quality of *The Jungle*.

2. Use the information you find to present a "pros and cons" look at *The Jungle* to determine the place you think *The Jungle* should have in American literature.

CliffsNotes Resource Center

The learning doesn't need to stop here. CliffsNotes Resource Center shows you the best of the best—links to the best information in print and online about the author and/or related works. And don't think that this is all we've prepared for you; we've put all kinds of pertinent information at www.cliffsnotes.com. Look for all the terrific resources at your favorite bookstore or local library and on the Internet. When you're online, make your first stop www.cliffsnotes.com where you'll find more incredibly useful information about Sinclair's *The Jungle*.

Books and Periodicals

This CliffsNotes book, published by IDG Books Worldwide, Inc., provides a meaningful interpretation of Upton Sinclair's *The Jungle*. If you are looking for information about the author and/or related works, check out these other publications:

BLINDERMAN, ABRAHAM (Compiler). *Critics on Upton Sinclair: Readings in Literary Criticism* (Readings in Literary Criticism, 24). Miami, Florida: University of Miami Press, 1975. Critical responses to *The Jungle* as well as other novels by Sinclair make this a good introduction to literary criticism.

BLOODWORTH, JR., WILLIAM. *Upton Sinclair*. Boston: Twayne Publishers, 1977. This biography provides an overview of Sinclair's life and serves as an excellent introduction to his work.

MOOKERJEE, R. N. *Art for Social Justice: The Major Novels of Upton Sinclair*. Metuchen, New Jersey: Scarecrow Press, 1988. This collection enables readers to compare *The Jungle* to some of Sinclair's other works of fiction.

SINCLAIR, UPTON. *My Lifetime in Letters*. Columbia, Missouri: The University Of Missouri Press, 1960. Sinclair's personal correspondences and commentaries provide insight into the private life and workingman behind *The Jungle*.

YODER, JON A. *Upton Sinclair*. New York: Ungar, 1975. A biography that provides an introduction to some of Sinclair's major works.

It's easy to find books published by IDG Books Worldwide, Inc. You'll find them in your favorite bookstores (on the Internet and at a store near you). We also have three Web sites that you can use to read about all the books we publish:

- www.cliffsnotes.com

- www.dummies.com

- www.idgbooks.com

Internet

Check out these Web resources for more information about Upton Sinclair, *The Jungle*, and Sinclair's other works:

The Jungle, http://www.ofcn.org/cyber.serv/resource/ bookshelf/jungl10—his site provides the entire text of Sinclair's novel in electronic form.

Literary Movements, http://www.gonzaga.edu/faculty/ campbell/enl311/litfram.html—in addition to providing information about literary movements and trends, this site provides a timeline so that you can see the historical events that occurred during Sinclair's lifetime.

Audio Recording

The audio recording of *The Jungle* can give you an even greater understanding of Sinclair's work.

The Jungle. (unabridged). Blackstone Audio Books, 1994. Although an abridgement exists, listening to the entire text, read by Robert Morris, is the only true alternative to reading the book.

Send Us Your Favorite Tips

In your quest for knowledge, have you ever experienced that sublime moment when you figure out a trick that saves time or trouble? If you've discovered a useful tip that helped you understand Sinclair's *The Jungle* more effectively and you'd like to share it, the CliffsNotes staff would love to hear from you. Go to our Web site at www.cliffsnotes.com and click the Talk to Us button. If we select your tip, we may publish it as part of CliffsNotes Daily, our exciting, free e-mail newsletter. To find out more or to subscribe to a newsletter, go to www.cliffsnotes.com on the Web.

Index

"I did not want—to do it", 91
"I will work harder", 16–17, 38, 91
"It's the second time they've sent me up on a trumped-up charge", 91
"When people are starving...", 65, 91
"You know what to do about it—vote the Socialist ticket!", 91

A

accidents determine fate theme, 38
aesthetics of novel, 87
African Americans, 64
alcoholism, 30, 43, 87
American Civil Liberties Union, Southern California branch, 5
American Dream, 25, 29
    loss of, 50
    original concept, 84
animal imagery, 17, 21
Antanas, 12, 36
    death of, 55
Appeal to Reason, 3, 8–9, 71
appearance versus reality, 21
Art for Social Justice: The Major Novels of Upton Sinclair (Mookerjee), 93
authorial intention, 8, 34, 89
Autobiography of Upton Sinclair, The, 4, 6

B

banking system, 38
Beef Trust, 22, 38
Bernstein, Eduard, 84
black culture, 63
Blinderman, Abraham, 93
Bloodworth, William A., Jr., 11, 93
Brass Check, The (Sinclair), 4
brothel, as symbol of capitalism, 65, 67
brotherhood, 85

C

capitalism, 18, 19
    alcoholism and, 87
    as violator of American values, 84
    cheating and, 40
    effect on family unit, 37, 78
    evils of, 21, 23–24, 48
    Sinclair's view of, 9, 65
    valuation of technology over humans, 42
chance, 71
character development, 17, 76
    lack of, 88
characters
    as stereotypes, 51
    author's abandonment of, 67
    exposition on, 20
    list of, 11–13
    types of, 9, 19, 76
children
    abuse of, 12, 17, 40, 48
    parental sacrifice for, 41
class consciousness, 58, 64
CliffsNotes Resource Center, 93
climax, 67
communism, 84
competition, criticism of, 22
Connor, Phil, 12, 45, 64
    as Jurgis' salvation, 82
    character analysis, 81
contemporary critics, 89
contrast
    factories versus forest, 21
    Marija versus Ona, 24, 36
    upper versus working classes, 59
corruption, 18, 26, 34, 40
    Connor as embodiment of, 81
    in judicial system, 47
    Jurgis' introduction to, 61
Critics on Upton Sinclair: Readings in Literary Criticism (Blinderman), 93
cultural criticism, 88–89
culture, 88

D

Dante, 85
Dede Antanas Rudkus, 12, 17, 26
    illness and death of, 30

democratic socialism, 84
disillusionment, 17, 26
Divine Comedy, The (Dante), 85
Doubleday, Page and Company, 3, 8
Doyle, Arthur Conan, 5
Dragon's Teeth (Sinclair), 2, 6
dramatization, 59
Dreiser, Theodore, 2
Duane, Jack, 12, 48, 61–62
   character analysis, 82
   It's the second time they've sent me up on
    a trumped-up charge, 91

E

economic slavery, 80
economics
   versus ethics, 39
   versus love, 32
election, 73–74
Elzbieta, 11
   character analysis, 81
   sacrifice for children, 41, 53
EPIC (End Poverty in California) plan, 5
equality, 85
exposition, 20

F

factories, as spoiled meat industry, 34
family
   journey to America, 20
   return to Widow Jukiene's house, 50
family unit, effect of capitalism on, 37, 78
fate
   determination by higher forces, 77
   good fortune from, 59
   shaping of, 18
fertilizer plant, 34
first person usage, 23
flashback, 20, 30
foreign words and phrases, 19
foreshadowing, 21, 25–26
   of dependence on Marija's income, 42
   of Jurgis' loss of Ona, 50
   of Jurgis' zeal for socialism, 32
   of means of survival, 31
   of Ona and Marija's becoming
    prostitutes, 37
free will theme, 9
Fuller, Meta, 3

G

graft, 8, 18, 34

H

Harper, Bush, 13, 61
Helicon Hall, 4
Hinds, Tommy, 13, 71
   You know what to do about it—vote the
    Socialist ticket, 91
hog allegory, 22
Holloran, Buck, 13, 61
house, 24, 26, 28, 29
   symbolism of, 25
hyperbole, 43

I

immigrants, 29
   plight of, 18, 26
   representation by Jurgis, 78
irony, 55, 58, 82

J

Jokubus Szedvilas, 20
Jonas, 11, 24
   disappearance of, 40
Jones, Freddie, 13, 59
journalistic technique, 35
judicial system, corruption of, 47
Jukiene, the widow, 12, 20
jungle comparison, 10, 31, 46, 61, 80, 85
Jungle, The
   critical reception of, 10, 88
   cultural criticism of, 89
   dedication of, 9
   endings of, 74
   historical impact of, 88–89
   naturalism in, 9
   objectivity, 9
   poetic license in, 8, 27, 35
   popular reception of, 4, 8
   publishers' debate over, 8
   publishing of, 3
   relevancy of, 10
   serial form, 8, 18
   socialist propaganda in, 10. *See also*
    socialism
   weaknesses of, 67, 71, 88

Jungle, The (audio recording), 94
Jungle, The Web site, 94
Jurgis, 11
  alcoholism of, 43
  Antanas, relationship with, 53
  attack of Connor, 45–46
  blacklisting of, 53
  character analysis, 77–79
  confrontation with Ona, 45
  directionlessness of, 50
  disillusionment of, 26
  epiphany in political meeting, 67
  exposition on, 20
  fanaticism about socialism, 71
  I will work harder, 16–17, 38, 91
  imprisonment of, 47, 61, 65–66
  individualism of, 77, 86
  introduction of, 17
  introduction to criminal world, 61
  jobs of, 22, 24, 41, 53, 55
  loss of innocence, 30
  losses of, 51
  meeting with Freddie Jones, 59
  naivete of, 21, 23, 78
  new life of, 57
  political involvement, 34, 61
  rebelliousness of, 61, 78
  sense of right and wrong, 78
  socialism, discovery of, 64
  socialism, transition to, 67, 69, 71,
    78, 85
  survival of, 57, 58
  suspicion of religion, 58
  symbolic journey through hell, 86
  transformation of, 47–48, 77–78, 85
  trial of, 48
  union involvement, 26, 32
  weakening of, 40

K

Kimbrough, Mary Craig, 4
Kristoforas, death of, 41–42

L

Lanny Budd series, 6
literary analysis, 87–89

literary devices
  animal imagery, 17, 21
  contrast, 19, 21. *See also* contrast
  hyperbole, 43
  journalistic technique, 35
  narrator, use of, 18
  second person, 18, 21
  time shifting, 18
Literary Movements Web site, 94
Lithuania, 16–17, 31
  versus Packingtown, 39
London, Jack, 2–3, 10
love
  between Jurgis and Ona, 28
  versus economics, 32, 80
Love's Pilgrimage (Sinclair), 4
Lucas, 13, 73

M

Madame Haupt, 13, 51
Majauszkiene, 28
Manassas (Sinclair), 3
Marija, 11, 24
  as foil for Jurgis, 81
  character analysis, 80–81
  character of, 17
  entrapment in capitalistic system, 65,
    73, 80
  injury of, 48
  job as beef trimmer, 36
  relationship with Tamoszius, 32
  similarity to Jurgis, 80
  strength of, 16, 32, 80
  versus Ona, 24
  When people are starving..., 65, 91
Marxists, 84
Meat Inspection Act, 8
meatpacking industry, 22
  corruption in, 26–27
  public perception of, 8
Moir, W.W., 3
money, dependence on, 29
Mookerjee, R. N., 93
morality plays, 78
muckraking, 10, 34, 62, 88
My Lifetime in Letters (Sinclair), 4, 93

N

narrative structure, 18, 88
narrator, 18, 76
    socialist agenda, 77
naturalism, 9, 77
naturalist practitioner, 9
naturalistic fiction, 43
naturalistic women, 79, 81
New Criticism, 87–89
Norris, Frank, 2

O

Oil! (Sinclair), 4–5
Old World
    Elzbieta as embodiment of, 81
    Jurgis' transition from, 67
Ona, 11
    character analysis, 79–80
    character of, 17
    death of, 51
    deterioration of, 40, 43
    difficult delivery of, 50
    employment of, 28
    exposition on, 20
    I did not want—to do it, 91
    prostitution of, 45
    return to work after pregnancy, 36
    strength of character, 79–80
    submissiveness of, 45
    versus Marija, 24
    weakness of, 36, 79
oppression theme, 20
Ostrinski, 13, 69
owners, 38
    greed of, 63
    power of, 53

P

packers. *See* owners
Packingtown, 22
    graft and corruption in, 18
    harsh realities of, 30
    life in, 17, 27
    tour of, 22
Packingtown swindles, 43
paradise, realization of, 86
point of view, 18
politics, corruption of, 35
power, 46

of money, 82
of owners, 53
process definition, 22
propaganda novels, 10
prostitution, 37, 43, 45, 57, 65–66
    Marija's acceptance of, 81
protagonist, definition of, 77
Pure Food and Drug Act, 8

R

realistic fiction, 65, 76
reality
    portrayal of, 9, 21
    versus appearance, 21
religion, 3, 5, 58, 86
rich own everything theme, 35
rural life, 57

S

Schliemann, Nicholas, 13, 73
Scully, Mike, 12, 34, 61
second person, 18, 21
setting, 9, 16
sexual politics. *See also* prostitution
    reversal of, 55
Sinclair, David, 3
Sinclair, Upton, 93
    agenda of, 8
    birth of, 2
    critical reception of work, 2, 5–6, 10, 88
    death of, 6
    early writing of, 2
    early years of, 2
    education of, 3
    historical view of, 85
    literary achievements of, 5–6
    literary career, 3–4
    marriages of, 3–4, 6
    political career, 5
    popularity of, 2, 4
    Pulitzer Prize for Fiction, 6
    pulp fiction by, 3
    religiosity of, 3
    social change, interest in, 2
    socialism, promotion of, 4–5, 10
social protest novels, 10
socialism, 4
    acceptance of message, 87
    as new religion, 86
    as savior, 69

as solution, 19, 78
implications of, 73
inquiry into, 87
Jurgis' first encounter with, 28
premise of, 84
rhetoric of, 23
Sinclair's promotion of, 9
socialist movement, 84
Springtime and Harvest (Sinclair), 3
Stanislovas, 12, 28, 40
    emotional death of, 30
stockyards, 16
strike, 63
style and language
    first person usage, 23
    foreign words and phrases, 19
    second person usage, 18
success, price of, 82
summary narrative style, 20, 63
    departure from, 67
survival of the fittest theme, 9–10, 30, 41
sympathetic characters, 23
Szedvilas, Jokubas, 12, 22

T

Tamoszius, 12, 32
technology versus workers, 42
tense, 18
texts, 88–89
themes
    accidents determine fate, 38, 46
    dependence on money, 29
    evils of capitalism, 40, 48, 62, 65
    loss, 51
    love second to economics, 32
    naturalistic, 9
    oppression, 20
    rich own everything, 35
    survival of the fittest, 30, 41
    women driven to prostitution, 31, 37,
        43, 45, 65–66, 79, 81
    work ethic, 38, 53
tone and voice, inconsistencies in, 88
tree analogy, 31
turning points, 51, 55

U

Uncle Tom's Cabin (Stowe), 10
union, 26, 32
Upton Sinclair (Bloodworth), 93
Upton Sinclair (Yoder), 93

V

Victorian novels, 76
votes, selling of, 34, 39

W

Warren, Fred D., 3
wedding of Jurgis and Ona, 16–18, 28, 30
Wilde, Oscar, 47
Willis, Mary Elizabeth, 6
women
    driven to prostitution, 31, 37, 65, 79. *See
        also* prostitution
    stereotypical representation of, 79
work ethic, 38, 41, 85
worker versus industry, 28, 32, 41

Y

Yoder, Jon, 93

Z

Zola, Emile, 9, 21
    definition of protagonist, 77
Zolaism, 21, 77
    departure from, 68

NOTES

CliffsNotes

LITERATURE NOTES

Absalom, Absalom!
The Aeneid
Agamemnon
Alice in Wonderland
All the King's Men
All the Pretty Horses
All Quiet on the
   Western Front
All's Well &
   Merry Wives
American Poets of the
   20th Century
American Tragedy
Animal Farm
Anna Karenina
Anthem
Antony and Cleopatra
Aristotle's Ethics
As I Lay Dying
The Assistant
As You Like It
Atlas Shrugged
Autobiography of
   Ben Franklin
Autobiography of
   Malcolm X
The Awakening
Babbit
Bartleby & Benito
   Cereno
The Bean Trees
The Bear
The Bell Jar
Beloved
Beowulf
The Bible
Billy Budd & Typee
Black Boy
Black Like Me
Bleak House
Bless Me, Ultima
The Bluest Eye & Sula
Brave New World
Brothers Karamazov

The Call of the Wild &
   White Fang
Candide
The Canterbury Tales
Catch-22
Catcher in the Rye
The Chosen
The Color Purple
Comedy of Errors...
Connecticut Yankee
The Contender
The Count of
   Monte Cristo
Crime and Punishment
The Crucible
Cry, the Beloved
   Country
Cyrano de Bergerac
Daisy Miller &
   Turn...Screw
David Copperfield
Death of a Salesman
The Deerslayer
Diary of Anne Frank
Divine Comedy-I.
   Inferno
Divine Comedy-II.
   Purgatorio
Divine Comedy-III.
   Paradiso
Doctor Faustus
Dr. Jekyll and Mr. Hyde
Don Juan
Don Quixote
Dracula
Electra & Medea
Emerson's Essays
Emily Dickinson Poems
Emma
Ethan Frome
The Faerie Queene
Fahrenheit 451
Far from the Madding
   Crowd
A Farewell to Arms
Farewell to Manzanar
Fathers and Sons
Faulkner's Short Stories

Faust Pt. I & Pt. II
The Federalist
Flowers for Algernon
For Whom the Bell Tolls
The Fountainhead
Frankenstein
The French
   Lieutenant's Woman
The Giver
Glass Menagerie &
   Streetcar
Go Down, Moses
The Good Earth
The Grapes of Wrath
Great Expectations
The Great Gatsby
Greek Classics
Gulliver's Travels
Hamlet
The Handmaid's Tale
Hard Times
Heart of Darkness &
   Secret Sharer
Hemingway's
   Short Stories
Henry IV Part 1
Henry IV Part 2
Henry V
House Made of Dawn
The House of the
   Seven Gables
Huckleberry Finn
I Know Why the
   Caged Bird Sings
Ibsen's Plays I
Ibsen's Plays II
The Idiot
Idylls of the King
The Iliad
Incidents in the Life of
   a Slave Girl
Inherit the Wind
Invisible Man
Ivanhoe
Jane Eyre
Joseph Andrews
The Joy Luck Club
Jude the Obscure

Julius Caesar
The Jungle
Kafka's Short Stories
Keats & Shelley
The Killer Angels
King Lear
The Kitchen God's Wife
The Last of the
   Mohicans
Le Morte d'Arthur
Leaves of Grass
Les Miserables
A Lesson Before Dying
Light in August
The Light in the Forest
Lord Jim
Lord of the Flies
The Lord of the Rings
Lost Horizon
Lysistrata & Other
   Comedies
Macbeth
Madame Bovary
Main Street
The Mayor of
   Casterbridge
Measure for Measure
The Merchant
   of Venice
Middlemarch
A Midsummer Night's
   Dream
The Mill on the Floss
Moby-Dick
Moll Flanders
Mrs. Dalloway
Much Ado About
   Nothing
My Ántonia
Mythology
Narr. ...Frederick
   Douglass
Native Son
New Testament
Night
1984
Notes from the
   Underground

The Odyssey
Oedipus Trilogy
Of Human Bondage
Of Mice and Men
The Old Man and
    the Sea
Old Testament
Oliver Twist
The Once and
    Future King
One Day in the Life of
    Ivan Denisovich
One Flew Over
    Cuckoo's Nest
100 Years of Solitude
O'Neill's Plays
Othello
Our Town
The Outsiders
The Ox Bow Incident
Paradise Lost
A Passage to India
The Pearl
The Pickwick Papers
The Picture of
    Dorian Gray
Pilgrim's Progress
The Plague
Plato's Euthyphro…
Plato's The Republic
Poe's Short Stories
A Portrait of the
Artist…
The Portrait of a Lady
The Power and
    the Glory
Pride and Prejudice
The Prince
The Prince and
    the Pauper
A Raisin in the Sun
The Red Badge of
    Courage
The Red Pony
The Return of the
    Native
Richard II
Richard III

The Rise of
    Silas Lapham
Robinson Crusoe
Roman Classics
Romeo and Juliet
The Scarlet Letter
A Separate Peace
Shakespeare's
    Comedies
Shakespeare's Histories
Shakespeare's
    Minor Plays
Shakespeare's Sonnets
Shakespeare's Tragedies
Shaw's Pygmalion &
    Arms…
Silas Marner
Sir Gawain…Green
    Knight
Sister Carrie
Slaughterhouse-Five
Snow Falling on Cedars
Song of Solomon
Sons and Lovers
The Sound and the Fury
Steppenwolf &
    Siddhartha
The Stranger
The Sun Also Rises
T.S. Eliot's Poems &
    Plays
A Tale of Two Cities
The Taming of the
    Shrew
Tartuffe, Misanthrope…
The Tempest
Tender Is the Night
Tess of the D'Urbervilles
Their Eyes Were
    Watching God
Things Fall Apart
The Three Musketeers
To Kill a Mockingbird
Tom Jones
Tom Sawyer
Treasure Island &
    Kidnapped
The Trial

Tristram Shandy
Troilus and Cressida
Twelfth Night
Ulysses
Uncle Tom's Cabin
The Unvanquished
Utopia
Vanity Fair
Vonnegut's Works
Waiting for Godot
Walden
Walden Two
War and Peace
Who's Afraid of
    Virginia…
Winesburg, Ohio
The Winter's Tale
The Woman Warrior
Worldly Philosophers
Wuthering Heights
A Yellow Raft in
    Blue Water

Check Out the All-New CliffsNotes Guides

TECHNOLOGY TOPICS
Balancing Your Check-
    book with Quicken
Buying and Selling
    on eBay
Buying Your First PC
Creating a Winning
    PowerPoint 2000
    Presentation
Creating Web Pages
    with HTML
Creating Your First
    Web Page
Exploring the World
    with Yahoo!
Getting on the Internet
Going Online with AOL
Making Windows 98
    Work for You

Setting Up a
    Windows 98
    Home Network
Shopping Online Safely
Upgrading and
    Repairing Your PC
Using Your First iMac
Using Your First PC
Writing Your First
    Computer Program

PERSONAL FINANCE TOPICS
Budgeting & Saving
    Your Money
Getting a Loan
Getting Out of Debt
Investing for the
    First Time
Investing in
    401(k) Plans
Investing in IRAs
Investing in
    Mutual Funds
Investing in the
    Stock Market
Managing Your Money
Planning Your
    Retirement
Understanding
    Health Insurance
Understanding
    Life Insurance

CAREER TOPICS
Delivering a Winning
    Job Interview
Finding a Job
    on the Web
Getting a Job
Writing a Great Resume